SACRED
ARCHITECTURE

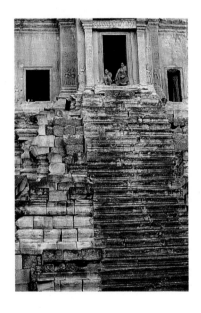

LIVING WISDOM

SACRED ARCHITECTURE

CAROLINE HUMPHREY AND PIERS VITEBSKY

SERIES CONSULTANT: **PIERS VITEBSKY**

Little, Brown and Company
BOSTON NEW YORK TORONTO LONDON

First American Edition

Conceived, Edited, and Designed
by Duncan Baird Publishers,
London, England

Editor: Kirsty Seymour-Ure
Assistant editor:
Ingrid Court-Jones
Designers: Richard Horsford,
Gabriella Le Grazie
Picture research:
Cecilia Weston-Baker

ISBN 0-316-38122-5

Library of Congress Catalog
Card Number: 96-78854

10 9 8 7 6 5 4 3 2 1

Published simultaneously in
Canada by Little, Brown &
Company (Canada) Limited

Typeset in Times NR MT
Color reproduction by
Colourscan, Singapore
Printed in Singapore
by Imago Publishing Limited

Contents

Introduction

In sacred architecture, humans attempt to bring themselves closer to the divine by creating a special space to hold this powerful and precious contact.

We are accustomed to thinking of sacred architecture in terms of magnificent temples, cathedrals and mosques which tower for centuries above the communities that built them. This is indeed a widespread means for humans to express their yearnings for the divine, and the use of expensive and long-lasting materials clearly reflects human longings for eternity. But eternity can also be expressed through the regular destruction and renewal of temporary structures, such as the wooden Shinto shrines at Ise in Japan (see pp.94–5) or certain Mesoamerican temples that seem to have been destroyed and rebuilt at the completion of every 52-year calendar cycle (see pp.62–3).

Although this book inevitably pays most attention to the monumental and long-lived architecture of the urban civilizations of Asia, Europe and Mesoamerica, it also includes examples from Africa, Native North America and Oceania in order to show that the construction of buildings for sacred purposes is a truly universal human activity. It does not depend on brick and stone, and even with the most short-lived constructions of mud and grass, the principles and meanings need be no different. A building's sacredness lies, not in the idea of permanence, but in the concentration of sacredness that it embodies or makes possible.

Many non-industrialized societies see the entire surrounding world as sacred, so that there can be no buildings that are not sacred. In many parts of the world there is no equivalent of the temple and all contact with the divine takes place in the open air or in the domestic dwelling. Even in societies with elaborate specialized sacred buildings, the house often retains a sanctity of its own.

The growth of specially designed sacred buildings was allied to very specific social and political developments. After many millennia of human religious consciousness, only in the last few thousand years have people devoted huge efforts and resources to the construction of monumental ziggurats, pyramids, temples and churches. In all cases this has happened as a result of the growth of the centralized state. Perhaps the gods had always been embodied in local chiefs and shamans, but now kings and emperors began to take on divine characteristics as part of their right and duty to rule. Conversely, deities came to resemble kings, and heaven itself became a royal city – still basic symbolism in Christianity today.

In the early kingdoms and empires of the Middle East, such as Mesopotamia and Egypt, the palace and the temple were the only monumental buildings and they were often not completely separate. But the balance between royal and divine power was often uneasy. In recent centuries, especially in Western Europe, kings have lost their divinity and the domain of the sacred has become limited to specifically religious institutions. However, the modern secular state has taken over many of the attributes of divine rule in order to retain control of its citizens (see pp.54–5).

Finally, "architecture" does not necessarily imply the existence of architects

The interior of Hagia Sophia (Saint Sophia) in Istanbul, Turkey. Built by the Byzantine emperor Justinian in AD532–7 to outshine the legendary Temple of Solomon in Jerusalem, the cathedral was converted into a mosque by Sultan Muhammad II on conquering the Christian city in 1453. In 1934, during Atatürk's secularization of the Turkish state, the building was turned into a museum.

in the modern professional sense. While building plans are known from early Babylonia and Egypt, and the principles of a long architectural tradition may be enshrined in treatises, as in India, it should not be forgotten that every hut or temple is the result of thought, planning and devotion and that much of the fineness of sacred buildings is owed to anonymous craftspeople. Ultimately, buildings are created by the whole of a society – or, as many believe, by the gods themselves, when they reveal the sacred plans to humans in dreams.

Architecture and the Cosmos

The design and construction of sacred buildings is the largest-scale form of art. It is surely also the most ambitious, as humans seek to re-create the realm of the gods on earth in a three-dimensional space that worshippers can enter physically as well as spiritually. Throughout the world, in diverse traditions and theologies, sacred architecture continually strives to reproduce the patterns, structures and alignments of the universe.

In some cultures, the sacred is isolated from the profane by the simplest of huts inside a fenced enclosure. In other traditions, magnificent towers, spires and *stupas* (domed Buddhist reliquaries) thrust upward to the heavens, giving material form to the spiritual journeys of mystics, shamans and saints. Many sacred buildings bring space and time together by providing an arena for the re-enactment of myths and rituals that link the beginning of time to the devotee's own present.

The ceiling of the Hall of Prayer for Good Harvest, Temple of Heaven, Beijing, China (1420), reproduces the geometric structure of heaven, according to Confucian belief. The hall was destroyed by lightning in 1889 and rebuilt to the original design. At the first ray of sun on the winter solstice, the emperor, who was the Son of Heaven, would offer prayers for bountiful harvests in the coming year.

Models of the cosmos

From earliest times, humans have believed that the cosmos contains more than the world immediately around them. The sky is often considered the realm of perfection, and the goal of much sacred architecture is to reproduce this perfection on earth.

Cities and temples are often believed to represent a form of heaven on earth. Jerusalem in Israel and Varanasi in India are considered holy cities because they are thought to reproduce a heavenly prototype. The Hindu temple at Sri Rangam in southern India was brought from heaven to earth, just as the Kaaba at Mecca (see pp.80–81) is seen by Muslims as an exact model of a heavenly temple.

The most compact model of the cosmos is the Hindu *mandala* – a diagram that represents the structure of the universe, which is used in rituals and as a meditational device. The *mandala*, as a ground-plan, underlies the temple throughout the Hindu, Jain and Buddhist worlds. It combines the circle (the original meaning of the word *mandala*), representing the celestial realm, with the square, representing the shape of the material world on earth. The sides are oriented toward the four cardinal directions, while a dot at the centre represents Mount Meru, the cosmic mountain and axis of the universe (see pp.22–3). In meditation the *mandala* is the basis for a mental journey toward the centre of the diagram, which is also toward enlightenment. In architecture it is used as the ground-plan of the temple, so that the temple reproduces the structure of the universe and also comes to function as a three-dimensional meditational device. At the centre of the tem-

A late 18th-century architectural thanka *(cloth painting) of Samye Monastery, the oldest Buddhist teaching monastery in Tibet, showing how the buildings are laid out according to the plan of a* mandala.

ple is the inner sanctuary, above which rises a tower symbolizing Mount Meru.

According to the idea of the *mandala*, numerous superficially different aspects of reality share a common form. The Buddhist temple of Borobudur (see pp. 24–5, 162) is laid out on a perfect *mandala* plan and is at the same time *stupa* (reliquary), altar, cosmic axis, centre of the world, body of the Buddha and teaching of the Buddha.

Many ancient civilizations believed that it was the reproduction of the structure of the cosmos in sacred architecture that made human life possible by pro-

THE HEAVENLY JERUSALEM

In the Hebrew Scriptures (Old Testament) the prophet Ezekiel was carried off in a vision to a high mountain, where an angel showed him the precise specifications of the future Temple of Solomon in Jerusalem. In the New Testament the idea of the heavenly city of Jerusalem is developed to represent a state of divine perfection which once existed on earth and which will descend again to earth at the end of time. Like Ezekiel, St John in the mystical book of Revelation is also taken to a high mountain by an angel with a gold measuring rod to contemplate the heavenly city of Jerusalem. But the "city" now means the community of Christian believers, united through Christ's offering of himself as sacrificial lamb. St John says, "I saw no temple in the city; for its temple was the sovereign Lord God and the Lamb". Even sacred buildings will vanish when their function is fulfilled through the person of Christ. There will no longer be any need for a temple as intermediary space for communion between the human and the divine.

The mosaic in the chancel of the 6th-century church of San Vitale, Ravenna, Italy. Christ is depicted as the Lamb of God at the centre of a starry sky – images symbolizing respectively the resurrection and the realm of heaven. Four angels support him, each standing on a globe.

viding a model for the laws of society on earth. This view applied to the city as well as to the temple and it made the spiritual and political dimensions of power virtually identical. In Mesoamerica, the city was often laid out as an exact model of a heavenly city. The Aztec capital of Tenochtitlán was constructed according to a divine ideogram (see pp.134–5), while at Teotihuacan (see pp.114–15), the entire city, containing thousands of temples, was itself equivalent to a great temple.

Similarly, Romulus founded the city of Rome by ploughing a circular furrow around the Palatine Hill. This circle was called the world (*mundus*) and was divided into four quarters like the cosmos. In historical times this legendary action was repeated at the foundation of every new Roman city, when a priest, or augur, would draw a circle on the ground and quarter it with lines running to the four points of the compass. The line from east to west represented the course of the sun, while the north–south line was the axis of the sky. By the use of prayers the augur would project this alignment outward over the whole area of the future city.

Celestial alignments

Stonehenge, England (c.2500–2000BC). Some scholars believe that the alignment of the stones can allow the accurate prediction of the movement of the sun and moon, including eclipses.

The alignment of a sacred building is rarely random. It may be aligned to a tree, along a river or toward the site of a holy event in the past. Perhaps most often, the building is aligned in relation to the trajectories of the sun, moon, stars and planets. Such an alignment may be crucial for making the building into a meeting point between the earthly realm of humans and the celestial realm of the gods.

Many sacred buildings, from Greek temples to megalithic passage-graves, face the rising sun as the source of new life and power. In most Christian churches a similar point is made. One enters from the west and progresses toward the altar at the east, moving from darkness to light and from death to life. Early English churches often deviate slightly from true east, a variance that can be traced to the position of the rising sun on the day of the saint to whom the church is dedicated. Sometimes accurate alignment is deliberately avoided, to create a special meaning. In some English cruciform churches, the chancel is skewed to represent the head of Christ falling sideways on the cross.

Celestial alignments seem to have become more elaborate with the growth of cities and empires. Ancient Chinese cities were laid out as a model of the universe, following a north–south axis that corresponded to the celestial meridian. At the centre, corresponding to the position of the pole star, was the royal palace. The city thus re-created the celestial order on earth, with the emperor as central figure. From Sumeria to Mexico, ancient cities repeatedly show a parallel between celestial alignments and centralized political power.

The relationship between astronomy and architecture was often sophisticated and precise, as can be seen in the alignment of Mesoamerican temples and observatories to the movements of Venus or the Pleiades (see pp.16–17). Similarly, it has been suggested that the narrow shafts in the great Egyptian pyramids may be aligned with the belt of Orion (see p.150).

Sacred buildings may also directly represent the year – in the traditional Vedic Hindu altar, 360 bricks stood for the days of the year (as they were reckoned) and 360 stones for the nights. Some buildings are designed as a calendar, as was probably the case with Stonehenge and the Big Horn Medicine Wheel in Wyoming, formed out of boulders on the ground. In Cuzco, the Inca capital of Peru, the Sun Temple was situated at the ritual centre of the city. Forty-one *ceques* (sighting lines) radiated from the temple, passing through significant sites which were both astronomical and linked with events in Inca history. The surrounding region contained 328 points along or adjacent to these sacred alignments, corresponding to the number of days in the Inca year.

THE PAWNEE EARTH LODGE

Among the Pawnee of the plains of North America, each village is said to have been founded by a star. A hereditary chief is that star's representative in the community. The circular earth lodge, the ceremonial centre of a village, is aligned with the cardinal directions and constructed according to mythical beliefs about the stars.

As described by the anthropologists P. Nabokov and R. Easton, the floor of the earth lodge is sunk three feet (one metre) into the ground. The lodge is approached down a slope and entered from the east, where a post represents the Morning Star, god of light, fire and war. A post at the western end represents the Evening Star, goddess of night. Each day, Morning Star shines his beam into the lodge through the entrance, repeating his first mating with Evening Star, from which sprang the first human. A post to the north is the North Star, the chief star; a southern post is the Milky Way. An altar at the west is the garden of Evening Star, where corn and buffalo are constantly regenerated. In front of the altar is the throne of the creator god Tirawa and at the centre of the lodge is a firepit – the open mouth of Tirawa, who enters the lodge in a shaft of light through the smoke-hole. Rituals are accompanied by sacred singing, which reaches its climax as this light moves across the interior and falls directly on to the fire.

A stylized plan of a Pawnee earth lodge.

Chichén Itzá, Mexico

GULF OF MEXICO

Chichén Itzá ●

■ Mexico
City

MEXICO

GUATEMALA

HONDURAS

PACIFIC OCEAN

Chichén Itzá is the greatest of the ruined Mayan cities of Mexico's Yucatán peninsula. The city was built by the Maya c.AD600–830 and was probably captured by the Toltecs in 987. It was abandoned c.1200, at a time of increasing instability and warfare.

Early cities and temples are often oriented in some way to the north–south axis, the pivot of the celestial drama of the movement of stars and planets. In ancient Mesoamerica, such orientation was extreme – sometimes entire cities were constructed as precise functioning astronomical instruments. Chichén Itzá, located in completely flat terrain, contains one of the best examples of astro-

nomical architecture – the mysterious asymmetrical Caracol observatory.

The astroarcheologist Anthony Aveni has identified distinct groups of buildings according to orientation, notably at 17 and 22 degrees east of north. These orientations are related to events such as the setting of the Pleiades, the rising and setting of the sun at the equinoxes, and the movement of Venus, conceived as the feathered serpent Kukulcan who dies as the evening star and is reborn as the morning star.

The shafts and openings of the Caracol enabled very specific astronomical sightings: all point in different directions. Mayan astronomers achieved astonishing results without the wheel, optical instruments or clocks, relying on architecture that, by means of devices such as slits in a wall, allowed sighting by eye.

ABOVE *A carved serpent's head at the base of the great pyramid of El Castillo (the castle), representing the god Kukulcan, the Mayan counterpart of the Aztec Quetzalcóatl (see also main picture, opposite).*
ABOVE RIGHT *The Caracol observatory gained its name (Spanish for "snail") because of its internal spiral staircase. A cylindrical tower on*

a two-tiered platform, the Caracol originally had six horizontal sight tubes or shafts, of which only three now survive. The ancient Mesoamericans were particularly interested in the movements of the sun and in the disappearance and reappearance of Venus, the bright planet whose associated god, Kukulcan, stood for warfare and blood sacrifice. Mayan astronomers used the

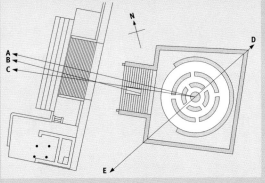

Caracol partly to demarcate significant points in the celestial path of Venus. Their extremely accurate calculation of the Venus year was based on data collected over 384 Earth years.

RIGHT *A plan of the Caracol observatory showing the major lines of astronomical orientation: (A) sunset at midsummer; (B) the northernmost setting point of Venus; (C) sunset on the day of the sun's zenith passage (that is, when the sun passes directly overhead); (D) sunrise at midsummer; (E) sunrise at midwinter.*

ABOVE *The pyramid of El Castillo was dedicated to the feathered serpent god Kukulcan. Just before sunset at the annual spring and autumn equinoxes, the sun picks out a wavy line along the sloping balustrade of the stairway on the shaded northern side of the pyramid. This line of light and shadow undulates directly down to the carved serpent's head (see opposite left) lying at the base of the staircase, and makes the serpent seem to come alive and descend from the temple – this was probably seen as a hierophany, or manifestation of the god. The four staircases of the pyramid have 91 steps each. Combined with the base step, this gives a total of 365, one for each day of the Mayan year.*

The cosmic pillar

A vertical axis linking this world with those above and below appears in systems of belief throughout the world in three dominant images. The World Mountain and the Cosmic Tree are probably the best known; the third is the Fire, with its column of smoke ascending to the sky. In architecture, the pillar often represents the archetypal cosmic axis, the centre line about which other objects rotate and to which they refer. Pillars may also express ideas that do not relate to the centre: ancient Greek columns, for example, may have symbolized sacred groves of trees where the gods dwelled. Cosmological significance is evident in numerous pillar forms, from the totem pole, the ritual ladder and the lotus stalk to the *lingam* (phallus) of the Hindu god Shiva; the cosmic pillar is also represented in spires and pinnacles, in an imagined line inside a building or in a thread from the highest point in the roof.

Such pillar imagery generally relates the earth (and sometimes an underworld) to the sky, but to be completely understood it must be interpreted in the cultural context from which it emerges.

The totem poles of the Native North Americans, for example, combine the image of the cosmic pillar with vivid and bold depictions of the sacred animal insignia of the clans to which they belong. Mounting to the sky, the totem poles declare the accumulated ancestral glory of the people who live in the houses below.

Images of a cosmic axis are particularly strong in Asia, where they can be traced back to the ancient Indian cosmology of Mount Meru, which stands at the centre of the world (see pp.22–5, 140–41). The Indian gods grasped this mountain-axis and used it to stir the primordial ocean, in this way initiating the creation of the universe. An important related image is the gnomon, the post that casts the shadow on a sundial. In ancient India, the gnomon was erected as a pillar and had two functions: it cast the shadows by which the true cardinal directions were

A totem pole of the Tsimshian people, British Columbia, Canada, depicting an ancestor and a winged creature symbolic of the clan. The upward thrust of the totem pole represents a link between the earth and the sky.

RITUAL TREES

Trees have been a recurrent inspiration for builders throughout the world, providing not only material for construction but a wealth of images: of verticality or solidity, of spreading branches, rising sap or life-giving fruit. The 1st-century BC Roman architect Vitruvius asserted that the first columns actually were trees.

The tree is a fundamental image in shamanic religions, in which a visionary specialist – the shaman – enters a trance-like state and is said to fly to other worlds where spirits dwell. In central Asia the ritual ascent is often described as "climbing the Cosmic Tree", whose seven or nine branches represent different levels of the universe. In North America, the Kwakiutl people of the northwest Pacific coast wrap a cedar "cannibal pole" in red-cedar bark to endow it with *nawalak* (supernatural power). Projecting through the roof of the house, the 40-foot (12-metre) post represents the copper Pillar of the World, which upholds the heavens. It is this post that the shaman climbs in rituals to reach distant realms of the universe. The pillar is also the insignia of the god Baxbakualanyxsiwae ("the man-eater at the mouth of the river"). Such associations between trees and deities or spirits occur also in the imagery of totem poles (see main text).

In modern Mongolian yurts the open hearth has been replaced by a stove, but the fire is still sacred and the stovepipe directs the smoke upward to heaven.

temple is built, therefore, it is a symbolic reiteration of the act of separation that allows life to proceed. As long as the primordial chaos is separated into distinct vertical parts, such as heavenly, earthly and the lower demonic realms, the world may continue.

established, and it was an architectural representation of the king of the gods, Indra, who "pillared apart" heaven and earth. Both Mount Meru and the gnomon are represented in the *shikhara*, the central tower of a temple. Each time a

The symbolism of the Inner Asian yurt (domed tent-dwelling) refers to a cosmology based on the cardinal points and a three-layered universe. Here the pillar is invisible, yet absolutely vital. The Mongolian yurt consists of felts

THE GOTHIC SPIRE

The main features of Gothic style are all vertical structures. Pointed arches, flying buttresses, rib-vault ceilings and spires are directed upward as if reaching toward heaven. These features first came together in 1144 in the revolutionary abbey-church of St-Denis near Paris. The first great Gothic spire was on the south tower at Chartres Cathedral (1194–1220). However, due to the difficulty, danger and expense of building them, many more spires were designed than were completed (Chartres was intended to have six, rather than its actual two).

Unlike the restful harmony of the Greek temple, the Gothic tower uses sharp tracery, interruptions of line and spiky pinnacles to express religious aspiration. The architectural historian Nikolaus Pevsner has written that Gothic architecture achieves a precarious balance between the vertical and the horizontal. The spire – the culmination of all the elements – represents a logical necessity to complete the effect of upward movement that starts at ground level. The balance and contrasts between the upward drive and the horizontal pull may be seen as reflecting the tension of the Christian soul striving for holiness.

The spires of Milan Cathedral (begun 1386) rise in a forest of pinnacles expressing the aspiration toward heaven.

PAGODAS

The pagoda is a Far Eastern development of the Buddhist *stupa* (see pp.104–5). The Chinese pagoda is attached to a temple, and has an image of the Buddha on the ground floor, beneath which is a crypt containing buried treasures. The pagoda may be hollow or it may have several floors, carrying a series of images or with one giant statue rising up through a number of stories.

The elegant series of ever-smaller roofs and balconies receding into the sky probably developed from the 13 discs or "umbrellas" that Indian *stupas* acquired around the 11th century. But the pagoda may have had a native antecedent in the domestic house: this was a single square room, over which was a study, and above

The 15th-century Porcelain Tower, Nanjing, was built by the emperor Yongle of brick and smooth glazed white porcelain.

that an attic granary.

Pagodas are often sited strategically to block the entry of evil spirits from the north-east – the direction from which devils are thought to appear. Cosmic significance may be indicated by an uneven number of floors – usually seven, nine or thirteen – relating to the number of skies in the universe. In recent centuries, pagodas have had several functions, from watching for enemies to announcing the pomp and power of town authorities.

The Japanese pagoda usually has five roofs widely overhanging a square base and is topped by a thin, many-layered finial (*hosho*), the sacred pinnacle of the temple. The pagoda is often surrounded by pine trees, whose silhouette it resembles.

tied over a round wooden structure of lattice walls and a roof made of poles radiating from a central ring. The outer ends of the poles are tied to the walls, while the inner ends are slotted into the central ring. Supported by two posts, the ring is left uncovered and functions as a smoke-hole. The line from the hearth through the smoke-hole to the sky forms the vertical axis, and it is from the position of the hearth that the four cardinal directions are reckoned. The hearth-fire is at the same time domestic and sacred. It is protected from impurities and aggressive actions, and symbolizes the ongoing life of the family. To say, "May your hearth-fire be extinguished", is the worst of evil spells, equivalent to wishing the extinction of

all descendants. Like smoke on a still day, prayers ascend to the sky, which is said to be the source of all blessings. The sky is said to receive sacrifices in the form of the vapours of meat cooked on the hearth.

The yurt is an example of an archetype – the domed hut at the ideal centre of the world, containing an axis to the heavens – that is found all over Asia, although the meanings given to it may differ. In ancient India a variant was the cupola on the central summit of the temple, such as at the 7th–8th-century shore temples of Mamallapuram in southern India (see p.140). The cupola represents both the hut of the wandering forest ascetic and the cap on the vertical shaft of the cosmic pillar.

Temples as mountains

Perceived in many faiths as the feature on earth that most perfectly aspires to reach heaven, mountains are often held sacred and are widely seen as the abode of the gods. Mount Kilimanjaro is sacred to the Masai of East Africa, as was Olympus to the ancient Greeks. Mount Kailash in the Himalayas is revered by Hindus, Buddhists and the followers of Bon-Po, the old shamanic religion of Tibet, and the four faces of Kailash bear a distinct resemblance to the mythical Mount Meru, with its four faces aligned to the cardinal directions.

An 18th-century gilt-brass model of Mount Meru from northern China. The centre of the Hindu, Jain and Buddhist universes, Mount Meru is surrounded by a concentric series of oceans, continents and heavens.

Even where mountains are not holy in themselves, they are potentially sites where gods may appear. In the Judaic tradition, Yahweh appeared to Moses on Mount Sinai. Sites such as this are often marked with a temple, as on the five sacred peaks of Taoism in China.

Just as the temple is a model of the cosmos on earth, so it may mirror the mountain that is the centre of that cosmos. In the irrigated desert landscapes of ancient Mesopotamia and Egypt, the temple was often built to echo the mythical mound of earth rising out of the primal waters (see pp.88–9). The word "ziggurat" (a stepped pyramid) derives from the Babylonian word for "mountain peak".

In some forms of the Hindu and Buddhist temple the idea of the cosmic

The step pyramid of Djoser at Saqqara, Egypt, one of the earliest pyramids (3rd millennium BC), consists of several stepped levels rising to a flat top. Its massive bulk dominates the surrounding desert.

THE MOUNTAIN AND THE CAVE

The symbolism of the mountain in Buddhist and Hindu sacred architecture is often combined with that of the womb (*garbha*) or cave. The Buddhist *stupa* has an inner chamber, called the cosmic "egg", emphasizing the regenerative qualities of the holy relic inside. The Hindu temple-mountain may contain cave-like spaces. In the temple of Parvati (*c*.AD465) at Nachna, Rajasthan, the outside walls are ornamented to represent piles of rocks and grottos full of wild animals.

The stupa *at Bodnath, Kathmandu, Nepal. The mountain-like outer shell is surmounted by a finial symbolizing the 13 Buddhist heavens.*

Examples of this hollow mountain-cave, with its connotations of the womb and promise of rebirth, are found throughout the world in the tomb, pyramid and mausoleum (see pp.144–57).

Beneath the Pyramid of the Sun at Teotihuacan, Mexico (see pp.114–15), is the womb-like sacred cave of an early people, which was probably thought by the later Aztecs to be their mythical origin point.

mountain gradually came to be expressed more explicitly. While the simple altar alone could symbolize the mountain, it was often enhanced by the addition of an altar terrace and a shrine or a *stupa*, and ultimately by the repetition of these features in diminishing tiers to form a whole temple. Such temples, with their repetitive ornamentation, resemble a range of mountains. Similarly, in Mesoamerica, several Mayan temples built on a single platform represented a range of mountains towering over the forest below (see pp. 112–13). At Angkor in Cambodia, the architectural arrangement of the temple signifies the concentric rings of the Hindu universe, dominated by Mount Meru at the centre. To emphasize its resemblance to Mount Meru, the base of the Baphuon temple at Angkor is concealed underground – as if, like the cosmic axis, the temple were simply passing through this world on its way from the lower world to the upper.

As a means for the soul's ascent toward the realm of the gods, the mountain may serve as the base for a further ladder, and even a small rock may be revealed as the base for the upward thrust toward heaven. The foundation rock of the old Jewish Temple of Solomon in Jerusalem now lies at the heart of the Muslim shrine of the Dome of the Rock (see p.141). This is the base from which the Prophet Muhammad climbed a ladder of light through the seven heavens into the presence of Allah.

Borobudur, Java

The Buddhist temple at Borobudur in central Java, begun in the 8th century AD, is probably the world's most elaborate architectural expression of the temple as mountain. Built on the summit of a small hill, it achieves its impact at close quarters, not from any intense skyward thrust, but from its immense mass, its ornamentation, and the subtly orchestrated progression of the visitor's ascent.

Like similar examples at Angkor in Cambodia and Pagan in Myanmar (Burma), the temple follows the ground-plan of a *mandala* (cosmic diagram), facing the four cardinal directions. A square base is surmounted by five square terraces, followed by three circular levels. The first four square terraces are surrounded by galleries of bas-reliefs in a vigorous style, while the circular layers are set with a total of 72 perforated *stupas* crowned at the top with a large, solid *stupa*. A stone staircase runs up the centre of each side.

The entire temple is an expression in stone of Buddhist metaphysics and doctrine and provides a visible and experiential aid to the believer's quest for release. The pilgrim does not penetrate inside the mountain, as with most Hindu and Egyptian temples, but ascends it on the outside, moving from illustrations of the world as we know it, to the level of inner vision on the upper terraces. The journey to the summit of the cosmic axis is also a journey to the ultimate insight of Buddhism.

ABOVE, ABOVE RIGHT AND OPPOSITE LEFT *The terraces of the temple contain a multitude of carvings. The square lower galleries of sculpture are designed to be circumambulated in an auspicious clockwise direction. The reliefs give a continuous narrative of stories from the various lives of the Buddha. (Here, the picture above right depicts the Buddha preaching to some disciples, while the picture opposite left shows a scene of mythical creatures.) The second to fourth levels depict the spiritual wanderings of the disciple Sudhana. At the end of the square terraces, as the pilgrim prepares to move on to the circular terraces with their dramatic change of architectural key, Sudhana enters the realm of the future Buddha, Maitreya, on Mount Meru.*

MAIN PICTURE, TOP *This aerial picture of Borobudur shows how the temple was built to the plan of a* mandala *(see p.162). As if meditating on a* mandala *the visitor ascends through different levels toward the highest – symbolizing the Buddhist* nirvana *(enlightenment).*

ABOVE RIGHT *On the circular levels, each stupa contains the statue of a meditating Buddha,* visible, although with some difficulty, through the stone lattice-work. The topmost stupa, at the axis of the universe, contained a statue (now lost) which was probably of the primordial Buddha (Adi Buddha), the ultimate source of the universe. This statue, which symbolized ultimate formlessness, would have been invisible to the pilgrim.

Dwellings of the gods

The sacred building expresses a fundamental paradox. The gods are the living force within everything on earth, yet they are not of this earth. They are both in their cult objects and icons (immanent) and beyond them (transcendent). They can be encountered in the sacred building, but although they may leave behind holy relics as objects of veneration and tokens of their presence, they cannot be contained within it. Sacred architecture is in part an attempt to capture a divine presence which by its very nature cannot be fully secured.

In monotheistic religions there is an emphasis on the formless, transcendent nature of God. This is most marked in Islam and Judaism, where the mosque and synagogue do not contain a representation of God, but focus worship on

The temple of Horus (237–57 BC) at Edfu. In ancient Egypt, the gods were believed to reside in their temples in a literal sense: the statue of the god, tended by priests in the inner sanctum, embodied its essence. The whole temple was a reflection of the glory of the god and, by association, of the pharaoh.

his cosmic law as written in a holy book (see pp.96–7, 108–9). In Christianity, although the church may be the "house of God", this is widely viewed as meaning not that God resides in a church, but that he can best be encountered there. Synagogues, mosques and churches are not a house for a god, like the shrines and temples of many other religions, but a house for God's people as a community of worshippers (see pp.42–3).

In polytheistic world-views, such as the Hindu or ancient Greek religions, temples accommodate different gods and serve in part to distinguish them from each other. Some religions combine notions of the gods' transcendence with more literal ideas of dwelling. Priests in ancient Egypt used to give the statue of the god in the inner sanctum a daily bath and feeding. In Japan, while the Buddhist temple is built to enclose a congregation, the Shinto shrine houses *kami* deities and often is not entered by the worshipper. But to the extent that they are present in this world, the gods are not equally present at all times or in all places. Even when they dwell in a sacred building, gods may visit it more intensely on special days and during rituals. The idea of a literal in-dwelling may be underscored by a ceremonial procession of a statue or holy relic around the temple, city or territory (see pp.76–9). This idea seems particularly strong when the temple is likened to a palace, from which the god emerges like a king or queen to tour his or her domain. Sometimes a statue may even be chained to its place in a temple during a siege to prevent its god from deserting the city.

HINDU TEMPLE SHRINES

In several Hindu traditions, deities such as Krishna and his wife Radha are represented in human form and consequently the temple becomes their house. The images are placed in shrines with doors and curtains to give them privacy at night and during their times of rest, with a miniature couch provided. Rituals represent each daily activity of waking, dressing, bathing and feeding the god, and the temple will keep an elaborate array of clothes and ornaments.

In larger temples the deities share their residence with their servants – the ascetics and priests – so there are dormitories within the compound, ranging from elaborately carved and painted wooden buildings in earlier centuries to modern apartment complexes. Guest-houses are set aside for visitors and provision is made for the large numbers of people who come for major festivals. Thus many temples have kitchens, dining-rooms and store-rooms, and some have cattle-stalls for the cows that produce milk for the temple. All food is first offered to the deities in small symbolic amounts, and is then eaten by the devotees as *prasad* (holy leftovers). The temple becomes a microcosm of sanctified human life.

A devotee brings offerings to a shrine of Krishna (Govinda) and Radha. Similar, although smaller, shrines are found in Hindu homes.

Choosing a site

A sacred site is a place marked out from ordinary space. A mountain-top or spring, for example, may be considered intrinsically sacred, as a focus of divine presence – many Hindu temples are built at a *sangam*, or confluence of two rivers, an especially auspicious location. Or a site may be made sacred by events that have occurred there, or by the carrying out of certain rites.

Humans often need a special sensitivity or skill to perceive the sacred nature of a site. The most elaborate system of divination based on latent natural forces in the landscape is feng shui, an ancient Chinese belief concerned with placing buildings in the most harmonious position in relation to their environment. This practice closely unites the spiritual properties of the land and of its buildings, influencing the choice of site not only for temples but also for graves, houses and offices. The Forbidden City of Beijing was sited and designed entirely according to feng shui principles.

Feng (wind) is associated with abstract and intangible forces, while *shui* (water) is connected with the tangible, physical environment. Feng shui practice examines the impact of these forces on each other. According to Chinese belief, the world is made up of positive energies, or *qi* (breath, air or current;

Feng shui experts use a special compass (lo pan) to analyze the position of a building, and from this a "birth chart" will be created for the site.

pronounced chee) and negative forces, or *sha*. The point of feng shui is to encourage the flow of *qi* and deflect the flow of *sha*. *Qi* is blown away by wind and carried by water, and too much of either will disperse good influences. Conversely, too little movement causes stagnation. If a house has been placed in an environment that is too still, people will install wind-vents or a fish-tank with running water to create a little disturbance. This is because the life-force of *qi* is not static, but moves constantly through the landscape, as it does through the human body.

Feng shui theory can be divided into the Compass School, based on astrological and numerological calculations, and the Form School, based on the significance of shapes and symbols. In practice, many experts often combine the two. The overall aim of feng shui is to create harmony and balance between exterior and interior forces, between humans and environment.

At the centre of Compass School theory is the principle of the five elements (wood, fire, earth, metal and water). Each element is associated with particular characteristics, linked to shapes in the landscape, to buildings and to individuals. The five elements correspond with the five directions (east, south, centre, west and north), which in turn correspond with astronomical animals and special colours.

In the Form School, the shapes of the landscape and of buildings in particular are paramount. Flat land with no undulations or hills is believed to be lifeless and lacking *qi*. The Chinese refer to hills or mountains as Dragons and Tigers

house with a narrow front but widening to the back signifies prosperity and many descendants. Acute-angled corners are thought to harbour stagnant areas of *sha* which may bring disease.

In other cultures too, special techniques may be used to enhance the sacred potential of a site. In the Kalahari Desert the Heikum Bushmen tradition-

Many of Hong Kong's buildings – including ultra-modern skyscrapers – are sited according to the principles of feng shui. A famous example is the Hongkong and Shanghai Bank (just to right of centre), designed by the architect Norman Foster in consultation with a feng shui expert.

(Dragons being the larger). The two are complementary, and it is important to identify both in a landscape. Buildings should be situated with a Dragon to the east and a Tiger to the west – the best location is when one hill continues behind the other, representing the Dragon and Tiger in an embrace. The ideal shape for buildings is a square, which suggests stability and endurance. L-shaped plots are seen as unstable. A

ally arrange their camp around a sacred tree which thereby becomes the central point of the camp's territory. The chief acknowledges the sacredness of the tree by building his own hut and lighting a sacred fire at the foot of it, while the other huts are arranged in a semicircle on the opposite side of the tree. In Hinduism, once a site is chosen for a temple, its specific natural features are transformed by the *vastupurusha mandala*

The Mahabodhi Temple at Bodh Gaya, India, was built at the site of the Buddha's enlightenment beneath the sacred bodhi *tree.*

(see p.36) into something cosmic and universal. A sacred site may even be reproduced elsewhere. The Egyptian temple represented a mud mound surrounded by water (see pp.88–9), and early reed temples were probably built on such islands rising out of the annual flood. But later stone temples were built on a solid foundation above the floodline even while their architecture elaborately imitated the original mud mound.

A site may become sacred through an event or action in mythical or historical time, and humans often respond to such an event by erecting a sacred building on the spot. Some of the most important temples to the Hindu Goddess stand at the places where parts of her body are said to have fallen after her suicide and dismemberment. Buddhism and Christianity have a strong cult of relics, and shrines are often built on the site of an event in the life of a significant figure. The locations of the stages and incidents of the Buddha's life are marked by *stupas*, just as sites associated with the lives and deaths of Christian saints and martyrs are marked by shrines. The first Buddhist *stupas* contained a relic of the Buddha's body, and the tombs of Christian saints may contain the saint's embalmed body inside an altar.

Religiously significant events often take place at sites that are already, as natural features, considered spiritually powerful. To build on the site is to hold on to its spiritual power and to prolong it through the continued existence of the building and the repeated rituals that take place inside it. Such repetition allows buildings to unite sacred space and sacred time.

A feature of some of the world's most powerful holy sites is the repeated reworking of the architecture on the same place, as buildings are enlarged or replaced. As a holy site focuses attention on the objects and actions it contains, it can become a spiritual magnet, leading worshippers to believe in an ever-increasing accumulation of sacred power. What starts as a modest shrine may grow as its efficacy is proven. This can happen dramatically at pilgrimage sites such as Lourdes, in France, which acquire a reputation for healing and granting wishes. The power of the visions experienced in the 19th century by St Bernadette is reaffirmed with each curing of a sick pilgrim under the three churches and magnificent basilica that now tower above the site.

The sacred power of a place can also survive and grow through architectural changes brought about by religious and political revolution, as one set of beliefs is rejected but the continuity of the site's power is acknowledged (see pp.156–7). The Soviet regime took over the spiritual aura as well as the physical fortifications of the Kremlin in Moscow. By building a stepped pyramid beneath the Kremlin walls for the embalmed body of Lenin, they placed a cult of relics at the heart of their new atheist state.

RITUAL HIERARCHY

A sacred building is often sited so as to dominate the community. From the European cathedral above the huddled parish to the chief's house-temple dominating the villages of Southeast Asia, the same theme is apparent. In the traditional culture of the island of Nias in Indonesia, villages are ordered according to an elaborate social hierarchy, headed by chiefs. The village is formed by the crossing of two large streets. At the central intersection are sacred foundation stones and megaliths, as well as the chief's house. In this culture there are no separate temples. Rather, people are under an obligation to increase their status by erecting stone monuments and holding feasts of merit – a ritual process that culminates in the building of a "great house".

The chief's massive house demonstrates visible ritual status above the whole community. The houses of the nobility are nearby, and are higher than those of commoners. Everything within the village – the layout and the style, height and positioning of the houses – vividly displays differences in social and ritual rank.

A view of a village on Nias, looking from the chief's house down the main street and processional avenue. The houses are more or less elaborately ornamented according to the status of their owners.

The mythical dimension

Myth interprets the present in terms of the past and is a way of explaining how phenomena in the world came to be as they are. The meanings behind the structure of a sacred building, as well as the rituals that take place within it, can be explained through myth. If the order of the temple mirrors the order of the cosmos (see pp.12–13), it is through myth that we learn how this is so.

A sacred building can serve as a location for the re-enactment of mythical events and the affirmation of the truths they represent. In Vedic Hinduism the consecration of the sacrificial altar re-enacts the creation myth. The clay in the foundation of the altar symbolizes the earth; the water with which it is mixed represents the primeval waters; and the side walls of the altar symbolize the atmosphere. In Christianity, churches provide a setting for rituals that commemorate the birth, crucifixion and resurrection of Christ at Christmas and Easter, while the Last Supper is repeated daily in the rite of the Eucharist.

Buildings can also embody or reflect myth in their very structure. Among the Dogon of Mali, each household's granary reproduces in its architecture the granary of the Master of Pure Earth who descended from the sky on the fourth day of creation. For the Dogon the granary represents a fertile female figure and the "belly of the world". In a further mythical correlation it is divided into eight internal spaces for storing the eight seeds that God gave to the eight ancestors, and to the eight internal organs of the body. These myths are reaffirmed in rites and in the respect shown toward grain in daily life. As with the Vedic altar or the Christian church, the religious meaning embodied in the Dogon granary is conveyed through narratives, or myths, that can be understood on many levels. The sacred building provides a map or point of reference

LEFT *This wooden granary door has been carved with a number of symbols and figures relating to Dogon myth.*
BELOW *A Dogon village in Mali with many typical thatch-roofed granaries.*

A kiva (ceremonial chamber) of the ancient Anasazi people at Pueblo Bonito in Chaco Canyon, New Mexico. Kivas are still used by Pueblo peoples such as the Hopi. A hole in the floor represents the hole through which the first people emerged in the Hopi creation myth, and is the focus for sacred rituals.

for such understandings, as well as a space within which to experience them.

Sometimes sites and myths converge. In Mesoamerica, the migrating Aztecs were told by their god Huitzilopochtli to search for an eagle sitting in a cactus and eating a snake: this was the sign that would identify the place where they should settle. They found the eagle on an island in Lake Texcoco, and there they built their capital city, Tenochtitlán.

In a similar way, the building of a temple is so highly charged with significance that designs are often seen as coming from a divine source. In ancient Iraq (c.2100BC), King Gudea of Lagash built the temple of the city's patron god Ningirsu after a dream: "Here was a man: his height equalled the sky, his weight equalled the earth ... He told me to build him a temple ..." This was Ningirsu, who revealed the detailed plan of the temple to Gudea. The king is often shown in statues of the period with the plan resting on his lap.

DAEDALUS

In Greek mythology, the architect Daedalus, imprisoned by King Minos of Crete in the labyrinth that he himself designed, escapes on wings of wax and feathers. Soaring above the labyrinth, he looks down on the tangle that baffles those who are still caught in it.

In this myth Daedalus escapes the limitations of the human condition and approaches the perspective of the gods. His son Icarus flies too high, has his wings melted by the sun and falls to his death, but Daedalus survives and returns to earth, because instead of being dazzled by the revelation of the labyrinth he absorbs its lesson. By understanding the architecture of humans, he also understands the architecture of the cosmos which it imitates.

Mayan ball courts, Central America

GULF OF MEXICO

Mexico City

Mexican Ball Courts

MEXICO

GUATEMALA

HONDURAS

PACIFIC OCEAN

Mayan civilization flourished until the 10th century. Mayan cities, like the cities of other Mesoamerican civilizations, had a ball court (*tlatchtli*), an open-air space dedicated to the acting out of a cosmic myth in the form of a ball game. This game was intimately associated with the belief, shared by other Mesoamerican peoples, that the sacrifice of human hearts and blood was necessary in order to sustain the movements of the heavenly bodies. The game was widely played for sport, but on ceremonial occasions war captives and foreign kings were forced to play and were decapitated when they lost.

Two teams had to keep a rubber ball passing back and forth, never touching the ground. The rules and the number of players varied, although usually players were not allowed to touch the ball with their hands and had to bounce it off their torso, hips and knees.

In Mayan myth, two twins, the world's best ball-players, disturb the lords of death in Xibalba (the underworld) with the bouncing of their ball. They are summoned to Xibalba, where they play against the lords, lose, and are sacrificed. Returning to life, they consistently outwit the lords in a series of deadly trials. Finally, they sacrifice the lords themselves and ascend into the sky, where they become the sun and the moon, forever setting and rising again. In other versions the twins are associated with the planet Venus, which is both the morning and the evening star.

ABOVE *A relief carving from the wall of the ball court at Chichén Itzá. On the left, a ball-player has been beheaded, and his torso is spouting blood. Similar carvings all around the ball court depict warriors, skulls and sacrifices. The heads of players were offered to the gods, and some carvings suggest that they may have been used as balls.*

OPPOSITE, MAIN PICTURE *The ball court at Copán has gently sloping sides with markers set into the centre of the floor. The transverse area in the foreground is a goal area.*
OPPOSITE, BOTTOM LEFT *The ball court at Chichén Itzá is the largest in Central America – nearly 500 feet (150 metres) long. The high vertical walls show influences from central*

*Mexico and suggest a different game from that played on the court at Copán. Huge stone hoops (*RIGHT*), fixed into the walls by tenons (wooden or stone projections), are set halfway between the two teams of players. The angle of the hoop deflected the ball rather than drawing it in, and even the greatest players would have found it difficult to score.*

Body, plan and proportion

Buildings have often been seen as reproductions not only of the cosmos but also of the human body. This correspondence may even be thought to constitute part of the building's sacredness. Megalithic tombs were sometimes constructed in the form of the human body, their inner space resembling the womb from which it was perhaps believed that the deceased would be reborn. The Greek temple complex at Delphi (see pp.142–3), like the Kaaba at Mecca (see pp.80–81), was called the navel of the world, while the Hindu god Shiva's phallus (*lingam*) is at the centre of every temple dedicated to him. Among the Dogon of Mali, the house plan represents a man lying on his side during the sexual act. The kitchen represents his head, the central room his belly and the grinding-stones his sexual organs.

The correlation between building and body is especially strong in some of the religions based on a key mythical or historical personage. The Christian church represents the body of Christ, who is himself divinity incarnate. The cruciform plan of many churches represents Christ's body on the cross. The priest celebrates mass at the head, where the blood and flesh of Christ are consumed.

Christ represents not only divinity

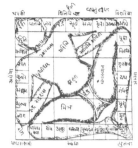

The vastupurusha mandala, *drawn on the future site of a Hindu temple, incorporates the human body, planets and gods and transmits their forms upward into the temple building itself.*

but also humanity, and in Byzantine churches the body symbolism is more generalized. The nave represents the human body, the chancel the soul and the altar the spirit.

A similar symbolism prevails in the Hindu temple. The classical Hindu temple is built according to the *vastupurusha mandala* – a diagram of 64 or 81 squares, in which the head, trunk and legs of the original cosmic man (*purusha*) are drawn; deities are placed in the various squares. A rite represents the planting of the "seed" of the future temple in the earth – a sacred area which will remain at the heart of the fully "grown" temple as the womb-like

The façade of the 15th-century church of Santa Maria Novella in Florence, Italy, was designed by the architect Leon Battista Alberti. Following Vitruvius, Alberti combined geometry and musical theory in the search for perfect harmony.

garbhagriha (inner sanctum). A related Hindu interpretation of the temple sees the entrance as the mouth, the dome as the head, the finial in the top of the dome as the suture in the human skull (the soft part of the skull that closes after birth), and the inner sanctum as the container of the human soul. The journey into this sanctum is therefore also a journey into one's inner self.

Often a sacred building literally contains the human body. Buddhist *stupas* enclose a relic, usually a portion of the body of the Buddha or a saint. Similar relics lie at the heart of many Christian shrines and churches, where bodily relics of saints and martyrs are enclosed in an altar, surrounded by the tombs of former worshippers.

The precise geometry of sacred architecture encapsulated in the *vastupurusha mandala* also occurs in other traditions. In the 1st century BC the Roman architectural theorist Vitruvius expounded an architectural geometry based on the proportions of the human body. His ideas were revived in 15th–16th-century Italy, where Roman remains were vividly present. Renaissance architects read Vitruvius so as to understand Roman architecture, and developed his ideas into elaborate theories of arithmetic, geometry and harmony.

In doing this, they largely rejected the medieval Gothic tradition, which had used a square-grid system that dated back through Rome to ancient Egypt. A spectacular example is the church at the abbey of Cluny, France (1080). The plan was based on a modular unit of five Roman feet and the modules were further grouped according to various theories of mathematical perfection, including Plato's succession by squares (1, 3, 9, 27 ...), and Pythagoras's series of numbers that were believed to underlie the structure of the universe as well as music and beauty in the arts.

LE CORBUSIER

In the 20th century, new proportional systems continued to emerge. The Swiss-born architect Le Corbusier (1887–1965) developed the Modulor, a modular system of standard-sized units, using a scale of proportions based on the human body and the Pythagorean golden section (a ratio between two dimensions such that the smaller is to the larger as the larger is to the sum of the two). Attacked for over-formalism in his apartment blocks, Le Corbusier confounded critics with his church, the Pilgrimage Chapel of Notre-Dame-du-Haut at Ronchamp, France (1950).

The interior of the church is a study in light. The thick walls are cut, often at an angle, by funnel-like openings with coloured glass windows. As the sun's angle changes, the space is transformed. Outside, the roof is a huge concrete boat-like shape, curving upward like a prow. Yet for all its freedom of form, the chapel is designed according to the Modulor.

Le Corbusier's church at Ronchamp, France. Its idiosyncratic shape defies the fact that it was designed according to strict formal principles.

Sacred and Social Dimensions

Religion concerns not only the relationship between humans and the divine, but also the relationships of humans with each other. Social relationships often follow divine models, and sacred buildings closely reflect distinctions between priests and laypeople, men and women, or dominant and subordinate political groups – frequently, buildings help to create and reinforce such distinctions. The structure of society itself influences the structure of sacred architecture. Through the way they are constructed, ornamented and used, sacred buildings also teach and reinforce religious understanding and beliefs.

The concept of sacredness is not limited to specially designed buildings. In many societies the domestic house is also sacred, being the centre of family life around the hearth and the focus from which sacred values are transmitted down the generations. Many societies have no separate temples, so that all their architecture is equally sacred, reflecting a sanctity that is inherent in the world itself.

A Kassena house, Burkina Faso. In Kassena society the building of a house is sanctified by foundation rituals performed by the "earth priest". The home is thus made a sacred domain for those who live in it. Built by men and decorated by women, it combines both male and female elements.

The sacred home

Domestic houses can be temporarily transformed into sacred spaces by the performance of rites within them, as happens in the Jewish home every Sabbath. This 14th-century Jewish manuscript shows a Passover meal.

The extent to which the home is considered sacred varies greatly among cultures. Modern Western society with its broadly secular outlook tends to focus ideas of sacredness on a specified area which is usually outside the home, and on an established priesthood: religion does not generally embrace all areas of life. In many traditional cultures, the distinction between secular and sacred is blurred or does not exist at all. But in any culture, a dwelling is a visible, material demonstration of an ongoing way of life, and as this is often felt to be the "right" way to live, so the dwelling may embody an order and ethical values that are deemed sacred.

In this way, even the domestic home can be used imaginatively to give shape to ideas. The house may be a physical model of another structure, such as the human body (see pp.36–7) or the cosmos (see pp.12–13). In other instances, more than just copying the structure of a person or an animal, the house is actually thought to *become* a body during rituals, when it is made to perform like a body. Among the Barasana Indians of Colombia, the longhouse is an ordinary dwelling-place for most of the time. At each end is a door, at one end for men, at the other for women, and a central corridor runs between the two. Each family has its hearth along the edges of the longhouse, and communal activities take place in the centre. But in rituals to convey mythic truths the house is personified as a mythical figure, an enormous bird called Roofing Father. The palm leaves used for roofing are his feathers. His head is at the male end of the house, his anus at the female end, and the roof-struts are his ribcage. The central male–female axis is

This 19th-century painting of a Sioux village by George Catlin depicts the tipi dwellings that were typical of the North American Plains peoples. Designs on tipis usually had sacred significance. Sometimes they were naturalistic, as here (a buffalo hunt), but Plains patterning often used symbolic geometric motifs such as the circle or the cross.

THE IGLOO

The igloo made of ice blocks is a temporary shelter found in certain regions of the Canadian Arctic. It reproduces a more widespread form of circular Inuit house, often underground, with a long narrow entrance passage for protection from the weather. In this society without separate temples, every aspect of the home has sacred meaning. For ritual purposes the igloo is likened to the womb and the entrance passage to the vagina. The domed roof represents the sky, the ice window the sun and the doorway the moon.

A typical igloo of the Canadian Arctic, with snowshoes wedged upright beside it in the traditional manner, ready for use.

his digestive tract, and the two doors represent the bodily openings for eating and defecation.

Variants of the same idea are found among many peoples, from Brazil and Central America to Indonesia and the Pacific. People may build a house to reflect the structure of the cosmos, as in the Inuit igloo (see box). By using their houses in ritualized ways – such as the acting out of the Roofing Father myth by the Barasana – people believe that they can control or change the processes in the cosmos.

In Southeast Asia the house is held to be "alive". In part this arises from the presence of a vital force suffusing everything: trees are thought to have their own wild power, which must be domesticated when they are felled for house-timbers. Among the Bugis of Indonesia each house has a "navel-post" where life-energy concentrates, and this post is dressed up to make it "look like a king". The Malays use the principle of "one house, one tree". The nine major house-posts are taken from a single tree-trunk and erected in the same order as they were cut, so as not to annihilate the tree's "life". Thus, the vitality of the tree continues in the house, and at the same time the ritual process of construction confers vital energy on the house.

With this background of belief, carvings are made as much for protection as for decoration. In Southeast Asia the house is a both a domestic home and a magical shrine. Its inhabitants are its soul, and its structure and carvings serve to protect that soul. Carvings must consist of flowing lines: a broken line may bring misfortune. If angered, a house can make someone ill, and there are healing ceremonies for offended houses. If a house is destroyed by fire and "dies", mourning rituals are conducted.

The sacred meeting-place

In many societies a meeting-house is a unique space because it creates a community and denies social divisions. But the meeting-house is frequently more than simply a place of assembly: it may be constructed for a sacred purpose, often defining the people inside specifically in relation to those outside. Thus the house may be an instrument in the construction of tradition and identity.

Among early Christians the meeting-house was a reaction to the pagan temple. During the first centuries, the Christians built no churches but used existing secular buildings for their meetings. Early Christianity was opposed to the combined power of state and religion, by which emperors and deities were worshipped side by side. The Christians' humble meeting-houses were places of prayer and communal faith; the underground catacombs in which they buried their dead were thought of as assembly places for the deceased. As the Church establishment grew, a specific architecture developed (see pp.124–5), but the ideal of spirituality manifest in a simple meeting of believers was constantly renewed. The Quakers (Society of Friends) have retained this ideal since the 17th century, and their meeting-houses are often in buildings of plain and secular appearance.

According to the anthropologist Nicholas Thomas, men's houses in Papua New Guinea unite all males, but their main purpose is as a place for rituals that teach boys an understanding of procreation and creativity. Much of cult life in Melanesia is motivated by sexual difference, and the men's house is symbolically opposed to the *bilum* (string bag) containing everything that epitomizes female life – from practical objects to amulets. The sharp-pronged, phallic images of male ancestors that are associated with the meeting-house contrast with the soft, rounded shape of the filled *bilum*, symbolic of the belly of a pregnant woman. Some meeting-houses loom 100 feet (30 metres) above ground. Their construction requires such technical feats that men regard the achievement of these buildings as miraculous and quite different from ordinary work. In this way the house is a form of magical art, and it

A Hotunui meeting-house, New Zealand, showing carvings of ancestors. The tongues protrude in a ritual gesture of challenge to outsiders, reinforcing the Maori sense of identity.

A Bororo village in Amazonia, with the men's meeting-house at the centre.

MEDIATING STRUCTURAL DIVISIONS

The men's meeting-house of the Bororo of Amazonia is built in neutral space at the centre of the village. Bororo villages are divided into two social moieties, or halves, and bisected by an east–west line. Men spend their adult lives in their wives' houses on "foreign" terrain (see p.53). The meeting-house mediates their strangeness, sited as it is across the territory of both moieties. It is a dormitory for unmarried men and a place of leisure for the married; it is where game is shared out and where rituals are performed. The village is a manifestation of cosmic order, with the men's house at the centre of a ring of dwellings arranged according to totemic clans. Through the meeting-house pass all transactions – both symbolic and material – uniting the various social categories that are differentiated around the edge of the village circle.

allows men to perceive their own creativity, which they define against the birth-giving fertility of women. Meeting-houses contain female as well as male symbols, and the enhancement of masculinity is in some sense based on mimicry of female creativity.

In New Zealand the *wharenui* (great house) of the Maori developed in the 19th century, given impetus by British colonialism. The *wharenui*, with its complex ancestor symbolism, enabled the Maori to assert their identity in a period of conflict and change. The building itself symbolized a general ancestor, and the elaborate carvings on the internal walls depicted ancestral heroes, with clubs, erect phalluses, bared teeth and extended tongues. The experience of the meeting-house was both a challenge to foreigners and enemies, and, for the men who identified with the ancestors, an affirmation of their own identity.

OVERLEAF *A meeting-house in the Sepik River area of Papua New Guinea. Through rituals that progress in stages throughout a man's life, this tremendous structure enables men to define and assert their identity in society.*

Priests and officiants

From the Egyptian inner sanctum forbidden to all but the priest, to the open hall of the mosque where the imam leads the congregation in prayer, sacred architecture and the role of the officiant are integrally related.

Officiants commune closely with the divine and may even be thought to enter the realm of the gods. In the Byzantine church, the altar is partly or wholly hidden behind the iconostasis (screen) in an area inaccessible to the congregation.

Monks at the monastery of Eihei-ji in Japan. The architecture of the monastery reflects the ethos of Zen Buddhism in its decorum and attention to function. The fish-like creature hanging from the ceiling is a drum that is beaten to call the monks to various duties.

As the priest passes through this screen of icons depicting heaven, he is said to become an angel.

Yet architecture must also cater for the needs of priests as mere mortals. Family life and communal life – or its absence – have a direct effect on architecture. Imams, rabbis and Orthodox and Protestant priests marry and live in family houses that are separate from the sacred shrine.

The rules of celibacy for priests, monks and nuns in certain religions lead to different architectural requirements and have varied consequences according to their relation to worldly power. Jain monks and nuns subsist on charity and donations and have little or no property. During the rainy season, they cease to move around the countryside and settle in the peripheral rooms of temples. They do not worship in the inner chambers since they have transcended the life of lay rituals, but they deliver daily sermons to a large lay audience in the temple's assembly-hall.

But in Tibet and medieval western Europe, Buddhist and Catholic orders built up monasteries that were vast economic enterprises rivalling the power of kings and emperors. The Rule of St Benedict states that a monastery should contain "water, mills, gardens and workshops" within its walls, and many Benedictine monasteries came to resemble small cities, with a church and chapter-house (administrative room) surrounded by their own bakeries, breweries, hospitals, farms and workshops.

While Greek Orthodox monastic communities such as those on Mount Athos (see p.59) retained familiar, hardly changing architectural forms, the monastic orders in western Europe became leaders in a succession of architectural styles, from the Romanesque of the Cistercians and Cluniacs to the Gothic of the Franciscans and Dominicans. Whereas many Greek monasteries maintained the early pattern of monastic life in which monks came together in a refectory to eat and then retreated to their separate cells, Benedictine monks read, prayed, ate and slept communally. They moved around according to a strict routine, and the plans and proportions of paths and cloisters were sometimes even designed to suit the length of specific prayers. The rules of monastic conduct invited constant improvement of the buildings for their fulfilment, as a perfect monastic life could be lived only in a perfect monastery. Architectural form and use were tightly related and the great medieval abbots were also usually the chief architects or planners of their buildings.

LIVING SHRINES

In many parts of the world, humans can be possessed by spirits or gods and themselves become a shrine. The spirits are said to dwell in the person just as if the possessed person were a building.

Some traditions have embraced symbols from new and foreign powers, which are often conceived of as spirits. These are represented in carvings or other "fetishes", where the spirits may be lodged and propitiated. The shamans or priests themselves temporarily become a shrine when the spirit enters: they then remove the spirit to the constructed shrine. Among the Fante of Ghana, such shrines are highly elaborate and iconographic, forming a focus of competition between rival *asafo* (military/social) groups. Along with traditional symbols, these shrines incorporate European images such as mermaids, clocks, machine guns and battleships.

A Fante asafo *shrine in Anomabu, Ghana, from 1952.*

Teaching the faith

For much of human history, teaching has been inseparable from religion, because the main lessons to be learned have concerned the meaning of life and the fate of the soul. Schools have usually been attached to the temple, mosque, synagogue or church. Their main purpose has generally been to train a new generation of priests and monks, who in turn would teach the faith to the wider lay population.

Architecture can enshrine reverence for the written word – for example, the Ark in a synagogue contains the scrolls of the Torah. But most populations at some time have been unable to read, and in some traditions buildings themselves became vast teaching systems filled with images intended to be understood at different levels by both educated and uneducated. Like the spoken and written teachings that they illustrate, such images are based on a repertoire of conventional emblems and gestures: St Peter holding the key to the gate of heaven, or the Buddha's hand-gesture calling the earth to witness his victory over Mara, the demon of ignorance.

The walls inside a Thai temple are painted with illustrations of the Jataka tales, describing the Buddha's former lives. The complex doctrines of suffering and rebirth are portrayed for an illiterate lay audience, using familiar pictures with no words. Images are placed in conventional locations where they are appropriate to the actions of the devotees who will contemplate them. The west wall is associated with death. There, behind the main Buddha statues, are reminders of mortality depicting the 31 ascending levels of states of existence from lower hells, through the human world, to heavenly states. On the north and south walls, rows of *devata* (deities) and benign demons sit in the same devotional posture as the human congregation. As devotees leave the temple via a doorway in the east wall, they gaze upon a mural of the enlightenment of the Buddha, as a reminder of the path to be followed in the world outside.

In this Thai Buddhist temple, Buddhapadipa, in London, England, the walls are covered with murals depicting scenes from the Buddha's life – a dazzling example of pictorial story-telling.

ARABIC CALLIGRAPHY

Arabic calligraphy is the highest of the arts of Islam, and it is said that a fine calligrapher will go to paradise. Whereas pre-Islamic culture had been a society of oral poets, the coming of Islam in the 7th century made it necessary to record and transmit the precise words of Allah. As Islam also discouraged figurative pictures, much creativity was poured into the development of script itself as an art-form. In architecture the basic motif is the repetition of the name of Allah, although designs also give the name of the Prophet Muhammad as well as verses from the Koran. The form and meaning of letters cannot be separated and the script can convey many layers of mystical teaching.

The dome of the Blue Mosque in Istanbul. Calligraphy makes the building itself into a medium for teaching the perfection of God.

In mosques, the avoidance of the portrayal of the human figure prevents the teaching of doctrine through pictures; the perfection of Allah is taught through geometrical design (see box). Other traditions combine geometry with images, creating a complex web of meaning. Medieval cathedrals in Europe served as elaborate encyclopedias in stone and stained glass, depicting the four apostles, the 12 months, the 12 signs of the zodiac, the four elements, the four rivers of paradise, the eight winds and the four cardinal virtues, all with a didactic purpose. The Royal Portal of Chartres Cathedral (1194–1260) was decorated with sculptures illustrating the seven liberal arts of arithmetic, geometry, astronomy, music, grammar, rhetoric and dialectic. The spectacular and highly formalized rose-window shows the souls of the damned being consigned to hell while those of the blessed are conducted up to heaven.

CHINESE SACRED MARTIAL ARTS

Many of the martial arts known in the West as kung fu evolved at Shaolin Monastery (AD495) in China. The floor of the hall was marked in squares, each identified with particular bodily postures named after animals and birds. Proceeding through increasingly sacred areas, the trainee had access to the entire space only after he had become a master. Architecture thus acted as a physical discipline which stood for a spiritual discipline.

Stained glass

The 16th-century east window of King's College Chapel, Cambridge, England. The chapel contains 26 stained-glass windows, and two-thirds of the entire wall area is glass.

Glass was invented around the 3rd millennium BC and was in use in ancient Egypt by *c*.1075BC. However, the use of stained glass in architecture is primarily a Western phenomenon. Techniques developed by the Syrians for making and colouring glass by the addition of metal oxides spread to western Europe between the 7th and 12th centuries AD, where it became the distinguishing art form of Christian architecture.

Stained glass gains its colour from light refracting through rather than reflecting off it, so that the colours change continually with the changing of the light. A stained-glass window is composed, like a mosaic, of pieces of coloured glass in a unified whole. The strips of lead that hold it together are an integral part of the design. As vehicles for spiritual expression, stained-glass windows combine pictorial story-telling with a sophisticated use of colour and light to influence feelings in the viewer. In the Gothic churches and cathedrals of the 12th and 13th centuries, the beauty of the medium was perfectly exploited, with structural developments such as tracery (ornamental stone patterns) and the flying buttress allowing whole walls to be made almost entirely of glass.

Like most religious art, stained-glass windows were intended to instruct by their subject matter, using recognizable imagery. Themes were usually taken from the scriptures and included scenes from the lives of Christ, the saints and the Virgin Mary, and depictions of vices and virtues. A distinctive technique was the juxtaposition of scenes from the Old and the New Testaments, called respectively types and antitypes. The type (Old Testament) scene was thought to prefigure the antitype, reflecting the medieval idea that biblical events were preordained. For example, Jonah's escape from the belly of the whale was believed to prefigure Christ's resurrection. Such scenes, taken from the devotional book *Biblia Pauperum* (Bible of the Poor), were a visual teaching aid, expressing complex theological ideas through allegory so that all people, even those who could not read, might understand.

TOP LEFT *A detail from the Adoration of the Magi, from a 16th-century window in King's College Chapel, Cambridge, England.*
TOP RIGHT *A roundel from the Miracles of the Virgin window at the 13th-century Chartres Cathedral, France.*
BOTTOM LEFT *A panel from the 12th-century west window of Canterbury Cathedral, England, depicting Adam after his expulsion from Eden.*
BOTTOM RIGHT *Stained glass has increasingly come to be used in synagogues. This window, from the Central Synagogue in London, England, portrays the Pesach Seder (Passover) table.*

Space and gender

The Hawa Mahal, or Palace of the Winds, in Jaipur, India, comprised five stories of lattice-like carved casements, which allowed segregated palace women to look out without themselves being seen.

A distinction between male and female spaces is often found in sacred architecture. Sometimes this only reflects one among a number of social differences evidenced in the building. For example, Anglican churches in northern India assign women to one side of the nave and men to the other, but they also place low castes at the back. Gender distinctions can also indicate different roles for the sexes in religion itself. In Orthodox Judaism women are allocated a separate gallery in the synagogue, reflecting the idea that men uphold ritual tradition while women's sacred duty is to ensure the continuity of the nation. In Islam, while the Prophet Muhammad had declared that women were equal to

men in the sight of God, by the Middle Ages women were seen as impure and were discouraged from attending the mosque; when they did attend they had to stand behind men in their own rows. Today, women still generally pray in a separate area of the mosque from men. In Christianity, early patriarchal images of God the Father and raised, separated spaces for male priests are challenged by the more egalitarian use of space in some churches and by women priests.

Gender distinctions may also be seen in domestic sacred architecture. Among the Kazakhs in Xinjiang, China, the yurt (tent-dwelling) is divided into male and female space; if a woman needs a utensil from the male side she will ask a child to fetch it. Because the yurt is a single open space, gender divisions appear in gestures, postures and the placement of one sex in relation to the other. By contrast, in certain Hindu and Islamic cultures, women's quarters are built structures. Women are secluded in a special part of the house, the zenana, which forms a complete world. Yet it is not entirely separate: grilles and tiny windows allow women to see without being seen, in an architectural analogy of the veil.

It is not always female space that is encompassed by male or undifferentiated space. Among the Bororo of Amazonia, women inhabit and inherit the houses in which they were born. Bororo society is divided into two halves or moieties, and an individual must marry someone from the other group. The layout of Bororo villages reflects this convention. It is men who go to live with their wives and who traverse the ideal line separating the two halves of humanity (see also p.43).

Structures themselves may be gendered. Tamil houses in southern India resemble the "living house" of Southeast Asia (see p.41): the house is "conceived" when its corner post, which signifies the male tree, is implanted in the female earth. This rite of implantation is symbolic of sexual union.

The wall of light, adjoining the hearth wall, in a Kabylie house near Tizi Ouzou, Algeria. The upright post is part of the woman's loom.

GENDER AND LIGHT

In North Africa, Berber houses relate the symbolism associated with light to the typical activities of each sex. The simple rectangular house of the Kabylie Berbers represents several complex and interlocking ideas of the sacred. The main door, symbolically male, is in the long eastern wall, faced by the smaller female door, set into the western wall. Lit by the sun coming through the male door, this wall, the "wall of light", is where women grind corn and do their weaving. Areas of darkness are female, and are associated with *haram* (taboo), with animality and nature (at the dark end of the house is a stable) and with sexuality, birth and death. Areas of light are male and are associated with the light and creative parts of the house.

According to the Kabylie, men are the light of the outside, public world, while women are the light of the interior. Men are expected to protect the domestic, creative activities of women, but they themselves must leave the house at dawn. Ridicule follows the man who spends time at home. To be inside, with their labour hidden, is the destiny of women. "A woman has only two dwellings," the Berbers say, "her house and her tomb."

Architecture and power

The emperor Constantine converted the Roman Empire to Christianity, and the Arch of Constantine (AD315) in Rome celebrates his victory over Maxentius "by the will of the Godhead", an ambiguous term acceptable to both pagans and Christians.

Architecture associated with powerful rulers often conveys an impression of sacredness. There are many reasons for this. Political and religious rule may be an indissoluble unity, as was the case in most early states – for example, in imperial China the emperor was considered to be the Son of Heaven. Even where church is separated from state, the church may remain enormously powerful, as is the case in Roman Catholic Europe. Conversely, a secular government may try to inspire awe by sacralizing its monuments, as in the 20th-century United States. In some cases, the secular buildings of an atheist power, such as ministries or universities, may be deliberately designed to compete visually with the religious buildings of the old order. In Soviet Russia, the pinnacles of Stalinist state architecture took over Moscow's skyline, which was previously dominated by churches.

Government buildings are not only working offices but also symbols of the state. They may be considered sacred if the state itself is perceived as such. This "sacredness" may appear in an overtly religious form (the Heian shrine-palace of ancient Japanese emperors), or by a quality of taboo (the Kremlin in Soviet times, which was prohibited to the public), or by both (the Forbidden City of the Chinese emperors in Beijing).

The architectural historian Lawrence Vale has noted how the Lincoln Memorial in Washington, DC, demonstrates sacredness and power. Architecturally it is a dramatic climax to the great avenue of the Washington Mall. Housing a 19-foot (6-metre) statue of Lincoln, the memorial is built in a classical, pillared design that recalls the Greek temple. To reinforce this association, a message is carved into the wall: *In this temple as in the hearts of the people for whom he saved the Union the memory of Abraham Lincoln is enshrined forever.* The open site, surrounded by a circular lawn, encourages access. Carved texts refer to the values of national unity, civil rights and racial equality for which Lincoln stands. Together, the meanings of the memorial establish a peculiarly North American concept of power.

Military might has been celebrated, from Roman times, by triumphal arches and processional routes. In Paris, the royal axis from the Louvre to the Arc de Triomphe is a famous example, although

OVERLEAF *The vast Potala Palace looms over the city of Lhasa in Tibet. Fort, palace and monastery, the Potala was the seat of the Dalai Lama, head of Tibetan Buddhism and former leader of the country. The building epitomizes the combination of temporal and spiritual power.*

its meaning has changed with history. During World War II it was a place of humiliation for the French as, in a daily ritual, the Nazis repeated their victorious march of 1940 along the Champs Elysées. In 1944 General de Gaulle returned along it in triumph. Now, the former ceremonial way of the kings of France links high art with advanced capitalism. The Louvre has been redeveloped with the architect I.M. Pei's glass pyramid, and the axis has been extended beyond the Arc de Triomphe in a line to the high-rise business district of La Défense, ending in J.O. von Spreckelsen's monolithic Grande Arche.

MONUMENTAL MESSAGES

Lenin's Mausoleum (built 1924–30) in Moscow's Red Square demonstrated the structure of power in Soviet Russia by the way it was used. At national festivals, serried ranks of Party leaders and generals stood high on a viewing platform on top of the tomb. On ordinary occasions, a long line of the "labouring masses" shuffled forward at ground level to the narrow entrance, where soldiers hurried them in and past Lenin's embalmed body.

Lawrence Vale has remarked how architecture allied with power almost always exudes contradictory messages. The buildings of great public institutions are subconsciously perceived as reinforcing qualities of stability, trustworthiness and order. Yet the buildings can also appear threatening: their scale and might remind citizens of their own powerlessness. Thus, messages of civic stability coexist with those of a more sinister, authoritarian

People line up outside Lenin's Mausoleum, waiting to be allowed in to view Lenin's body.

nature. Even in times of change, architecture can be used to reinforce power, as buildings usually last longer than political reputations. For example, after Stalin was denounced in 1961, his body was removed from Lenin's Mausoleum so that the tomb might continue to signify the power of the Soviet state.

Retreat and isolation

Certain religious traditions exalt the spirit and place an intense value on contemplation of the other world, often at the expense of the flesh and material substance of this world. In architecture this has contradictory consequences. The withdrawal from this world by the hermit or monk seems to imply a disengagement from architecture altogether. Yet monasteries may be large institutions and are often centres of wealth and power – a fact that is demonstrated by their magnificent architecture.

The hermit's shelter may be deliberately more basic than even the poorest ordinary dwelling – the Greek sage Diogenes lived in a barrel, and for millennia Christian, Buddhist and Hindu hermits have dwelt in caves. Such isolation may be combined with an exaltation, or rising, toward God. St Simon Stylites spent most of his life on top of a pillar which supported a small platform just large enough to allow him to sleep. In early Christian Britain, isolated hermits' cells and chapels were built on inhospitable islands in the sea.

In many cultures, from Native America through East Africa to New Guinea, isolation is a temporary phase in almost everyone's life. Adolescents are isolated singly or in a group in a special hut in order to reflect on spiritual truths. While ordinary houses are often divided into male and female, senior and junior spaces, the simple structure of the initiation hut reflects the abolition of all previous social status. Since initiates are in the process of becoming a new social entity, the hut often resembles a womb, from which they will be reborn as adults. In parts of southern India and the Brazilian Amazon, girls

These Buddhist hermits' caves in Afghanistan are carved into the sheer rock-face and watched over by a stylized statue of the Buddha.

are secluded during their first menstrual period. Among the Dyak of Borneo they are isolated for a year in a white hut; they are also dressed in white and allowed to eat white food only.

As a lifelong vocation, monasticism is especially highly developed in Christianity and Buddhism. Large numbers of men and women withdraw from the life of sexuality, family and mundane economics, to pray for a world that will not pray for itself. In both religions this is linked to a theology in which salvation or *nirvana* is hindered by the distractions of the material world and of the flesh. Early monasteries grew to become the major social institutions of their society. The Buddhist monastery began as a retreat for contemplation, and developed into a large centre of learning, as in the early Buddhist university at Nalanda in Bihar, India. In Tibet, Buddhist monasteries became landowners and administrative and economic centres, as did Christian monasteries in medieval Europe (see pp.46–7).

MOUNT ATHOS

The first monastery on Mount Athos, northern Greece, was built in AD961. By the 14th century there were some 40 monasteries; about 20 are still inhabited, by monks of the Orthodox Church. No female is allowed on the peninsula – it is considered the exclusive territory of the Virgin Mary.

The monasteries are built as fortresses, with massive wooden gates that are locked at sunset. Inside are extensive courtyards, each with its own church. In a cenobitic ("life in common") monastery, the monks hand over all property and eat together in a collective refectory. In an idiorrhythmic monastery they retain their own property and the architecture enables them to live and eat separately.

Outside the monasteries are *sketes* and *kellia* – small huts lived in by two or three monks. Beyond these are the cells of the strict hermits, who live outside the monastery system altogether. A hermit's dwelling may be just a ledge or a hole in the cliff-face. Other monks lower food to them in a basket but never see them or exchange a word. If one day the basket is not emptied then they know that the ledge is available for another inhabitant.

Simonas Petras monastery: typically, the wooden balconies of living-quarters project high above fortified lower walls.

A map of Mount Athos dating from the 1960s. The area is also known simply as to aghios oros, *the Holy Mountain. The hermits' cells are mainly located on the precipitous cliffs of the southeast coast.*

Ritual and Ceremony

A sacred building comes into a relationship with human worshippers through ritual action. Rites of consecration and purification make the building into a suitable meeting point between humanity and divinity. Within this space, the meeting is generally enacted through the central religious act of sacrifice (whether literal or symbolic), which is also developed and elaborated in other kinds of action such as praying and dancing. These human deeds are matched by actions of the gods, who grant favours and bless worshippers within the arena of the building. This two-way communication intensifies the sacred power of a site, sometimes turning it into a magnet for pilgrims who come, often at enormous personal cost, to seek a transformation in their lives at this proven gateway to the gods.

The annual festival of Pooram is held in the town of Trichur in Kerala, southern India, in April or May. The festival honours the two principal goddesses of the town. The main deity of each of the two temples (Thiruvambady and Parammekkavu) is carried by the central elephant of each party of 15 elephants, all richly adorned and carrying ceremonial umbrellas. In the evening the elephants of the Parammekkavu temple line up outside Trichur's most famous temple, the Vadakkumnathan, dedicated to Shiva. Thousands of devotees come to Trichur to celebrate the festival, which includes processions around the temples and ends with a spectacular display of fireworks.

Consecration and purification

The consecration of a building is the creative or ritual act that transforms a mere material structure into a functioning link with the divine.

The rite of consecration may symbolically repeat the creation of the cosmos, as is seen in many societies from ancient Sumeria onward, or it may be a form of taking possession. This is the case with the consecration of a Roman Catholic church, where each phase of the ceremony isolates the building further from the secular world and brings it into the realm of Christ. The bishop circumambulates the church three times, stands on the threshold and makes the sign of the cross, and then after entering banishes evil with holy water and sanctifies the building with prayer. As a final act of possession, a relic of the saint to whom the church is dedicated is installed in the altar, establishing a direct historical as well as spiritual link to Christ.

In Hindu temples the physical repositories of spiritual power are not relics but images such as statues, which are treated as if they were the gods themselves. Images, like buildings, require consecration to convert them from the product of an artisan into a divine reality. Hindu statues may be consecrated by prayer and by offering them food and sprinkling them with water. In Sri Lanka and Thailand, statues of the Buddha are consecrated by painting on the eyes. This is when the spirit enters in, a moment considered so dangerous that the painter uses a mirror so as not to be caught in the spirit's direct gaze.

Animal sacrifices are often made in the course of construction. In Yoruba regions of West Africa, before the central house-pole is erected an animal is ritually slain, its blood poured around the site and its body placed in the posthole. This consecrates the foundations by ensuring the benign presence of the spirits and by repelling any evil powers that may be at the site.

Once a building has been consecrated it must be protected from pollution, and this is often achieved through regular rites of purification. Some Mesoamerican temples were rebuilt at every

The traditional dwelling, or hogan, of the Native American Navajo is the centre of family and spiritual life. Hogans are usually consecrated several times a year with the Blessingway chant (see p.134). The chant refers back to the original hogans built by the gods of sunrise and sunset, and reinforces the hogan's sacred and symbolic meanings.

INCENSE

In numerous cultures, temples and houses are purified by the burning of aromatic herbs – these are considered to please the gods and to drive away demons. True "incense" is made from frankincense, the resin of the *Boswellia* tree, and was widely used in Greek, Roman and Jewish temples. Early Christians condemned incense as a pagan custom. During the Roman persecution of Christians they were ordered to burn incense before a statue of the emperor as a test of loyalty; many were martyred for refusing. But its use in the Church grew from the 5th century onward, and among non-Protestant denominations incense plays a major role in purification.

A Coptic priest at the church of the Holy Sepulchre in Jerusalem waves a censer with purificatory incense.

renewal of a 52-year calendrical cycle. Many Hindu temples are purified and rededicated every year.

Such rites may be echoed on a small scale in daily worship. Worshippers should be in a pure state of body and mind, and mosques and Shinto shrines in particular provide special areas for washing before entering. The purity of the Shinto shrine is often further protected by three bridges over three streams which the worshipper must cross in a progressive purification.

The act of consecration can be reversed or annulled. Conquerors desecrate the temples of their enemies through impure or insulting actions. Redundant churches are deconsecrated before being turned over to secular use, and it is possible that the great temples at Teotihuacan in Mexico were deconsecrated by being burned down (see p.114).

Consecration and purification reveal very clearly the analogy between a building and the human body (see pp. 36–7). The consecration of a priest is similar to that of a building, and in monastic traditions the consecration of the individual and the maintenance of a state of purity become a way of life.

Sacrifice and offerings

Sacrifice is a religious ritual in which an object or a life is offered to a divinity in order to establish a desired relationship between humanity and the sacred order. It has been found in the earliest-known forms of worship and in all parts of the world. Many bloodless symbolic rituals refer to an archetypal sacrifice involving killing – the offering of a physical life in return for a life-sustaining blessing. Just as sacrifice itself is a complex phenomenon, the architecture connected with it takes many forms.

In some societies that have no separate temples, sacrifices are conducted in every home. In West Africa, an altar may be built in each family's compound, often in the shape of a dome, which is sprinkled with the blood of chickens sacrificed to the ancestors. These altars are a point of contact with the ancestors, fulfilling the same basic function as a temple or church elsewhere.

This basic similarity is not always appreciated when different religions come into contact. When the Catholic Spanish invaded Mexico in the 16th century they found a powerful Aztec civilization based on large-scale human sacrifice. The sun god Huitzilopochtli required a constant supply of human hearts in order to allow the life-giving sun to cross the sky. At the Templo Mayor in the capital Tenochtitlán (see pp.112–13), priests dragged their human victims up steep steps to the top of the pyramid where Huitzilopochtli's temple stood. The victims were stretched backward over a sacrificial stone and their hearts, still beating, were cut out. The priests then flung the bodies down the steps – thus re-enacting a mythical victory of the sun over his sister the moon,

whose dismembered body was depicted in a carving at the base of the pyramid. The consecration of the Templo Mayor in 1487 is said to have involved 20,000 victims, although such figures are probably exaggerated by the Spanish to defend their moral right to the Americas.

In Asia, sacrifice played an integral part in the rulers' exercise of divine power. In China, elaborate sacrifices to heaven and earth were offered by the

MINE DEVILS OF BOLIVIA

Tin-miners in Bolivia believe the precious ore they seek moves around underground and can conceal itself or yield itself to the miner at will. The ore is controlled by powerful spirits which resemble the Christian devil and are the true owners of the mountains where the ore is found.

As with the harvesting of animals in hunting societies, the extraction of the ore is a privilege that must be paid for in a form of exchange. If the spirits are not properly appeased by regular offerings they can cause catastrophe and death underground. Effigies of the mine devils are placed at specially constructed shrines in the mine, and it is to these that offerings are made, typically consisting of coca leaves, cigarettes and alcohol. Some shrines are simply excavated out of the rock, others echo the styles of the religious architecture of the area in an amalgam of Catholic and pre-Christian pagan traditions.

This shrine in Potosí, the main mining town of Bolivia, has been dug out of the rock; offerings are strewn before the effigy of the mine devil.

An Aztec chacmool figure forms an altar below the Temple of the Warriors at Chichén Itzá, Mexico (see pp.16–17). Sacrificed human hearts are believed to have been placed on the flat plate he holds.

emperor. They took place in Beijing on the Altar of Heaven, three marble terraces surmounted by the round, triple-roofed Temple of Heaven, built in 1420 on the site of an earlier sacrificial mound. The imperial sacrifices set in train the seasonal processes of the weather and fertility that would ensure the harmony and success of the empire. In southern China, a different kind of sacrifice was practised, connected with the cult of ancestors. On the death of an emperor, hundreds of his subjects were killed and their bodies placed in or near his tomb (see pp.146–7). The blessing of

imperial ancestors would be forthcoming only if they were properly accompanied by servants in death as in life.

In present-day Nepal, Hindu sacrifice unites all citizens in the defeat of demonic forces. In Bhaktapur city, the whole town acts as an arena for the drama of sacrifice, in an annual ritual in which intoxicated water-buffalo (they are given alcohol to drink) are chased through the streets to the temple of Taleju, where they are slaughtered. The city comes to a halt and police hold up traffic for the stampede. Facing the entrance to the temple is a statue of its

The ornate gateway to the temple of Taleju in Bhaktapur, Nepal. The buffalo sacrifice takes place in the courtyard.

represent not only external evil but the sins committed by the citizens which must be expiated. Similar sacrifices take place all over Nepal.

In many religions blood sacrifice is transformed into a symbolic form or replaced by other offerings. In early Judaism, rites of atonement on the day of Yom Kippur involved animal sacrifice at the Temple in Jerusalem and the sprinkling of sacrificial blood in the inner sanctum by priests, in order to annul the Jewish nation's sins and obtain divine forgiveness. This rite now takes the form of a day of repentance, with rituals and prayers in the synagogue. In Christianity, the complex theology of Christ's sacrifice – the shedding of his blood to atone for the sins of all humanity – is reflected in elements of church architecture. While the rite of communion is central to Christian worship, only the Catholic Church retains its sacrificial terminology – the doctrine of transubstantiation asserts that the bread and wine are literally the body and blood of Christ. In Catholic churches, therefore, the altar (where communion takes place) is prominent. The Orthodox Church views the communion as a life-giving encounter with the resurrected Christ: this is reflected in the celestial domes of the Russian tradition depicting the risen Christ. For Protestants, Christ's sacrifice was unique and all-sufficing, so that repeating it in ritual is unnecessary; Protestant

founding king, seated on a pillar. Taleju is the goddess of the regional royal lineage, and although the kings of Bhaktapur no longer reign, still their representatives (priests or officials) must chop off the heads of the buffalo before the public. The 24 buffalo – one for each part of the city – symbolize the demonic armies. By killing them the priests demonstrate victory over evil and celebrate the divine-kingly rule that preserves both the natural and the moral order. This sacrifice also contains the idea of the scapegoat. The buffalo

THE ALTAR

The altar is a structure on which sacrifices are offered. Originally probably no more than a mound of earth, a rock or a heap of stones, altars became more elaborate with the development of sacrifice as an element of worship in temples. In the book of Genesis, Abraham builds an altar on a mountain, on which he lays his young son Isaac, as he prepares to make the burnt offering by which he is tested by God. Biblical sources also detail altars covered with goatskins and cloth.

In the Christian tradition, altars notably take the form of a table, contrasting with the solid block of pagan altars. Often covered with cloth, the Christian altar also evokes the table of the Last Supper. Many altars have become elaborate, incorporating an altarpiece (a structure above the altar table adorned with holy images) or a reredos (a screen fixed to the wall behind the altar). Although the altar itself

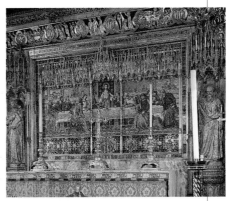

The reredos and altar at Westminster Abbey, London; the altarcloth evokes the biblical table.

is usually plain, the altarpiece and reredos have inspired some of the greatest painting and sculpture in the Christian tradition.

churches are places not of cultic rite but of commemoration of Christ's teaching.

Offerings are prominent in those religions that have rejected killing. In Bud-

dhism and Jainism, temples and shrines commonly have altars in front of the divine images for symbolic offerings, which include oil lamps, incense, money, sweets, fruit and flowers. The offerings are made in a ritual, *puja*, in which gifts to the god are combined with prayer, meditation and chanting. *Puja* is also widespread in Hinduism, where it may include blood-sacrifice; in the non-violent traditions, it is a "sacrifice", but one that entails the giving up of wealth. This mirrors the relinquishing of worldly things by the original ascetic teachers. Thus, paradoxically, the temples of the Jains, who emphasize the spiritual merit of asceticism and poverty, contain the greatest heaps of offerings laid before the images by the devout.

A Hindu man performs puja *at a household shrine in Kerala, southern India. He is making an offering at the door of the rice-store to ensure that the rice gods remain benign.*

Praying, preaching and dancing

Praying, the expression of a wish, plea or attitude, is the central act of communication from humans to the divine. Sacrifice, offerings and even the construction of buildings can all be seen as a form of prayer. A building is not necessary for prayer; but it is repeated prayer that keeps the home sacred, as when Hindus set aside a pure shrine-room for praying or Christians say grace before a meal. Among Jews, Sabbaths and festivals are initiated

A muezzin (crier) sends his call to prayer out over the landscape surrounding this village mosque in Turkey.

by a ceremony in the home as God's name is praised over wine and bread, and candles are lit to signify God's presence in the house.

A specially designated sacred building

comes into being at a location where repeated prayer is believed to be most necessary or efficacious. This may be around a tomb, where one prays to or for the dead, or a shrine, where one prays to a saint. When a building is designed for prayer, the interior architecture will closely reflect the form of service offered to the divinity. For example, Islamic theology and prayer require very little differentiation of internal space (see pp.96–7).

Preaching and reading from holy texts are a form of communication from the divine through a human intermediary. Preaching can take place in the

THE MUSLIM PRAYER-RUG

In societies that are traditionally nomadic, the prayer-rug functions as a portable mosque, providing a ritually pure space wherever one finds oneself on the trail. The patterns on the rug help the worshipper focus on the eternal truths of Islam. There is usually a representation of the *mihrab*, the niche facing toward Mecca (see pp.96–7). Sometimes this is abstract, a square surmounted by a triangle. The square symbolizes the material world, the triangle the spiritual realm. The sides of the triangle represent man's contemplative ascent to God or the descent of God's grace to man.

The border round the rug defines the boundary of this pure space and its contact with the outside world. This contact is often expressed by interlocking reciprocal designs. In the North African desert, nomadic Tuareg who have no mat may trace an outline of a mosque in the sand and step inside it to pray.

A prayer-rug from Tabriz, Iran. Every rug contains a deliberate mistake – only Allah is perfect.

open air, as when Christ preached to a crowd on the Mount of Olives or the Buddha preached his first sermon to five ascetics in the Deer Park at Sarnath (a site now marked by a *stupa*). Where a building is designed for preaching or readings, as in Islam, Judaism, Sikhism and Christianity, the interior takes the form of an auditorium. Even against the background of an egalitarian theology, its use will often reflect fundamental social distinctions, not only between clergy and laity but also within society at large. In the Sikh *gurudwara* (temple) the congregation often listens to readings sitting on the floor, with men and women on separate sides. In the mosque, men prostrate themselves in an egalitarian way but women are often segregated. Among the Buryats of southern Siberia, Buddhist *lamas* sit in rows below their standing congregation. The Western Christian church generally has wooden pews arranged in formal rows. This can allow a reflection and reinforcement of the social hierarchy, with the best seats reserved for local notables, a practice repeatedly rebelled against by egalitarian Christian movements.

The architecture of preaching and reading also emphasizes desks, lecterns and pulpits. The Christian pulpit may be of wood or stone, a separate structure or a niche or projection in the wall. It occurs not only in churches but also *(text continues on page 72)*

OVERLEAF *A white-robed congregation sits in rows on the floor of the Great Temple of the Cao Dai sect in Tay Ninh, Vietnam. Founded in southern Vietnam in 1926, this sect includes the Buddha, Confucius, Christ, Joan of Arc and Victor Hugo in its pantheon of saints.*

The pulpit in the Baroque cathedral of St Stephen, Bavaria, is high above the congregation, showing the importance of preaching in the Church tradition: from here, the priest's voice will carry clearly.

in many monastery refectories, where the monks eat in silence while listening to a sermon or a reading. Occasionally a pulpit overhangs the street, as in the church of Notre Dame at St Lô in Normandy. In Islam, a pulpit of tamarisk wood, mounted up two steps, was built in the Prophet's mosque at Medina, Saudi Arabia, during his lifetime (c.AD 570–632). The ruler tried to remove it to his own mosque in Damascus but was deterred by an eclipse of the sun which signified Allah's disapproval. Instead, he raised the pulpit by a further six steps to the height it commonly has today.

Where a procession is important to a religion (see pp.76–9), the building will encompass corridors or paths, as in the Egyptian temple, or a nave or ambulatory, as in the Christian cathedral. If there are cult secrets, there will be an inner sanctum protected by ante-rooms

from the approach of the uninitiated.

The path-like form of the Egyptian temple leads to the secret inner sanctum, whereas in the Christian cathedral the nave leads to an altar. Far from being secret, the altar is the central and most conspicuous part of the building because of the communal nature of Christian worship, especially in Roman Catholic buildings with their emphasis on the rite of the mass. Nevertheless, the altar is marked off as the most sacred

A prayer-wheel at a Buddhist monastery in Ulan Bator, Mongolia. Prayer-wheels are inscribed with or contain a consecrated text – each turning of the wheel is equivalent to reciting the prayer.

GREEK DRAMA

The gestures and emotions of prayer can be expressed and enhanced by specialists such as the *devadasis* (handmaids of the gods) at some Hindu temples, whose ritual dances give pleasure to the gods. Such rituals can also lead to the development of specialized architecture. The semicircular theatre of Greek drama, with its raked stone seats, was designed to allow thousands to witness the acting out of myths at the spring festival of the god Dionysos. The circular space (orchestra) at the centre had an altar in the middle, around which dancers moved singing prayers, accompanied by a flute.

The idea of a separate actor playing a mythical character emerged from the role of the chorus-leader. By the classical period (4th century BC) the texts were scripted by writers. Actors would enter for each episode, talk to each other to carry the story forward, and then exit; between episodes the chorus would sing and dance their emotional response. It was only later that drama gradually changed from religious ritual to entertainment.

The 4th-century BC theatre at Epidaurus is the best-preserved Greek theatre, and is still used for performances today. Even a whisper from the orchestra can be heard in the back row.

area of the building. An English Protestant church generally places it in a raised area called the presbytery ("place of the elders"), to be used during services only by the priest and perhaps the choir. An Orthodox church usually shelters the altar behind a screen of icons (iconostasis), beyond which no unbaptized person is allowed. Where the worshippers are not accommodated in the building, as in Greek and Roman temples, the altar is outside and becomes the focal point of public activity, while the less frequented interior has little need for elaborate functional divisions of space.

A sacred building can embody the regenerative aspect of prayer as it continually re-creates the cosmos. Each day in the dark inner sanctum of the Temple of Amun at Karnak in Egypt (see pp. 90–91), the priests tended the statue of the creator god Amun with its erect phallus. The god was believed to masturbate and give birth to himself anew each morning in a re-enactment of creation, and the reliefs of musicians and dancers surrounding the statue were perhaps thought to stimulate him. The priests looked after Amun on behalf of the pharaoh, whose greatest service to the god was to build for him.

Sound in space

There is a discernible qualitative difference between music heard in the open air and music heard inside a building. In a free space, sound travels outward, becoming less intense, until it is lost. In a building, sound waves are repeatedly bounced off surfaces in cross-cutting patterns. In a church the congregation hears not only the direct sound from a choir but also a conglomerate of weaker sounds that have been reflected before they reach people's ears. These multiple reflections are delayed in time in strict accordance with the distance travelled. Bare stone reflects nearly 100 per cent of sound energy; rough wood, soft materials and – above all – people absorb energy and return less than 25 per cent of sound to the audience. Architects have known such facts from early times, and, depending on the roles of speech and music in a given religious tradition, sound was controlled by the way in which a sacred building was designed.

In traditions emphasizing music, reverberation (the tail of reflected sounds heard after a note) is important. Human hearing merges sounds arriving within about 1/30th of a second of each other and registers them as one: reverberation effects an enrichment and prolongation of a sound. Stone cathedrals with pillars and high roofs produce a mixture of close and distant sound reflections, and long reverberations can occur. Churches were built to make this possible – much sacred music was written to accommodate the reverberations of particular buildings. Resonant space is also suited to the organ, which from the 9th century was almost exclusively a church instrument. Organ pipes sound for as long as a note is held down, then stop. Reverberations soften and "sanctify" such

BELL TOWERS

Christian bell towers were erected to call the faithful to prayer, but they came to serve many other functions. In medieval Italy, where the Church was a powerful political entity, bell towers (*campanile*) were often freestanding, to emphasize their elegant civic dominance, with arcaded stories and decorative brickwork. Visually – and so politically – they competed with the fortified towers of secular bodies which also pierced the city skyline.

Bells were imbued with diverse powers. Until recently, the tolling of bells was believed to protect the souls of the dead from evil spirits and to avert pestilence, and was used to warn of approaching storms. A 15th-century German bell bears the motto: *vivos voco, mortuos plango, fulgura frango* (I call the living, I lament the dead, I break up lightning).

The freestanding campanile *(bell tower) of Florence Cathedral, 14th century.*

Buddhist monks at Samye Monastery, Tibet, chant their prayers at a service. The hall is richly decorated with cloth hangings and silk paintings that absorb sound.

abruptness. Thus the cathedral itself may be seen as an instrument of sound.

Concave walls focus sound; instead of reverberations they produce discrete repetitions distinguishable as echoes. An apse produces this effect, and a dome can intensify it. The baptistery at Pisa, Italy, is famous for its echo: an arpeggio (distinct notes) sung there sounds like a chord (notes played together) and takes almost 25 seconds to die away.

By contrast, speech requires clarity, achieved by uninterrupted sound waves from speaker to audience and a short reverberation time. This is why pulpits are elevated above the congregation, and it is partly why Methodists and other faiths emphasizing the spoken word tend to build small chapels rather than vast, echoing churches.

Non-Western religions have different traditions relating sound to architecture, with less stress on reverberation and more on clarity. Much Eastern sacred music is performed in the open, or under a canopy. Temple music is an important tradition in Tibetan and Mongolian Buddhism, but hangings, wooden ceilings and silk paintings restrict reverberation and produce a dry, clear sound; horns, drums and clashing cymbals give periodic emphasis to the monks' chanting. The more ascetic religion of Jainism places importance on the spoken word, and Jain preaching-halls are plain and rectangular.

Procession and pilgrimage

From very early times, architecture has been designed to allow processions. As long ago as the 6th century BC, the main street of Nebuchadnezzar's Babylon was the Processional Way, along which statues of the gods were borne to the gate of the city's goddess Ishtar. Both procession and pilgrimage highlight a focal point of sacredness, in which a site or a building serves as a meeting-point between the human and the divine and as a source of power on earth. Often humans move toward the source of this power, as when worshippers approached the house of the god in a Greek or Roman temple. But they may also carry this power with them in the form of a statue or relic. A procession thus links separate places by creating a corridor of sacredness. Once the destination has been reached, people may deposit the sacred object, bear witness, or make a sacrifice or offering.

Processions may also lead out from a sacred building, when a divine power that ordinarily resides there goes out to the world. Once a year in ancient Egypt, when the Nile was in flood, the statue of the god Amun at Karnak was hidden in a cloth and taken on a barge upstream to Luxor. There, the pharaoh and his wife were secluded in an inner room with the statue, perhaps to perform a ritual sexual act in a rite that also renewed the pharaoh's divinity.

Throughout the Hindu world, gods may set out from their temple on an annual procession around their domain. The Temple of the Sun near the shore at

One of the 24 carved stone wheels on the Temple of the Sun at Konarak, designed in chariot form.

PILGRIMAGE AND CHURCH DESIGN

The ideal Christian pilgrimage in medieval Europe was to Jerusalem. But Muslim hostilities in that region made this difficult and many pilgrims visited other places instead. The roads were thronged with groups travelling to holy sites such as Canterbury, Santiago de Compostela and Cologne (locations of the bones of St Thomas Becket, St James and the Three Wise Men respectively), and to numerous local shrines with their proliferation of saints and relics. Churches were redesigned with more and larger aisles, naves and apses to hold greater crowds of pilgrims and processions. From modest prayer-houses for monks and congregations, they became huge reliquaries and eventually great cathedrals.

Local replicas were also built of the Church of the Holy Sepulchre at Jerusalem, where Jesus was supposedly buried. In this way the local worshipper could go to "Jerusalem" in a spiritual journey that was sometimes also represented by a maze on the floor (see p.139). These churches were not accurate architectural reproductions, but used architecture to embody the spiritual meaning by imitating the tomb and the round shape of the original.

During the 18th century, Baroque architects built "sacred stairways", so that the approach to a church was itself imbued with spiritual significance. Rome's Spanish Steps, ascending to the church of Santa Trinità via three flights of steps and three landings – representing the Trinity – are perhaps the best known.

Konarak in Orissa, India (built 1238–1264), was even designed as a massive chariot, flanked by 24 carved stone wheels and pulled by seven colossal stone horses. The remote jungle shrine of Kataragama in Sri Lanka brings Hindu, Buddhist, Muslim and aboriginal Vedda pilgrims to a group of temples which are little more than plain rectangular rooms. The temple of Kataragama houses the god in the form of a magical geometrical design (*yantra*) – a star in the shape of two interlaced equilateral triangles – on a small sheet of gold, which is seen by no mortal except for its keeper. The pilgrims watch as this *yantra*, wrapped in cloth, is escorted in a procession of elephants from Kataragama's own temple, down an avenue lined with the temples of other gods, to the temple of his mistress, the aboriginal jungle goddess Valli

Climbing the steps to the church of the Bom Jesús near Braga, Portugal, pilgrims pass representations of the Stations of the Cross and thus follow the stages of Christ's journey to his place of crucifixion.

Amma. He spends 15 minutes closeted with her, in commemoration of their original encounter when the god first arrived from southern India. In other parts of Sri Lanka the tooth of the Buddha and statues of the Virgin Mary are carried out from temples and churches in similar processions (*pera-hera*), though with different theologies.

Tours by gods are also a form of circumambulation, a movement around a place which they thereby sanctify or protect. Worshippers can also circumambulate, using their own body to create a circle. In Hinduism this must be done *pradakshina*, in the direction of the sun's movement, with one's pure right hand facing the revered object. Movement in the opposite direction is associated with death and sorcery. One may circumambulate one's guru, a temple before entering the inner sanctum, a holy city such as Varanasi, or even the whole of India. Buddhist *stupas* frequently have a special path around the outside, as in the terraces at Borobudur (see pp.24–5).

Procession and circumambulation are often the culmination of pilgrimage, undertaken to a place such as a tomb, shrine or monument that has a special spiritual value. The soul's progress toward union with that value may be reflected by the physical hardships of a journey across unknown territory, while the architecture of the

destination may reflect the purpose of the pilgrimage and the impact of arrival. The pilgrim to Lourdes, France, comes for healing and finds an arrangement of enclosed pools for plunging into the icy water of the miraculous spring from the nearby grotto where St Bernadette saw her visions of the Virgin Mary in 1858. The baths and the grotto lie at the foot of a cliff over which towers the Domain of Our Lady, a complex of three churches crowned by the spire of a basilica. The pilgrim to Varanasi,

This procession will circumambulate the Ruwanweli Dagoba at Anuradhapura, Sri Lanka, winding the cloth around its base.

India, comes to bathe in the holy river Ganges and often, for many sick and elderly pilgrims, to die at this most sacred place. The river is lined for three miles (five kilometres) with broad steps, backed by a cliff-like array of shrines, temples and towers. Funeral pyres blaze day and night and the ashes are cast into the river to enable the soul to attain a favourable rebirth.

Pilgrimage sites develop networks of transport, lodging and ancillary buildings and are often surrounded at festivals by temporary fairs and booths. At Kataragama (see p.77), cave-dwelling Buddhist nuns come out of their jungle caves in the pilgrimage season and give spiritual consultations to pilgrims at the foot of the "Milk Stupa" (*kiri dagoba*).

The relationship between buildings and faith is complex. The shrine of St Thomas Becket, martyred in Canterbury Cathedral, England, in 1170, was destroyed in 1538 by Henry VIII, who needed 26 wagons to remove its treasures. Yet even without the shrine, the cathedral remains one of the main pilgrimage sites in Europe. The treasures of the Greek temple of Apollo in Delphi were similarly plundered by Roman emperors (see pp.142–3). Today there are few if any worshippers of the Greek gods, but many visitors to Delphi still experience an immense spiritual power.

The tower of the huge cart of the god Jagannath resembles the Orissa style of temple tower.

THE RATHAYATRA FESTIVAL, PURI

Jagannath is a form of the Hindu god Krishna, and his temple at Puri in Orissa is one of the four most sacred pilgrimage sites in India. Every year the god's statue, along with those of his brother Balabhadra and sister Subhadra, is pulled through Puri in a procession of carts to commemorate Krishna's journey from Gokul to Mathura. The exalted raja of Puri sweeps the road in front of them, performing the actions of low-caste sweepers. Before hundreds of thousands of pilgrims, the procession travels from the main temple of Jagannath to the Gundicha Mandir (Garden House) nearly a mile (1.6 kilometres) away. After a week, the gods are pulled back to the temple.

The carts (*ratha*) are a work of portable architecture in themselves. The main cart of Jagannath is 46 feet (14 metres) high and has 16 wheels, each over six feet (two metres) in diameter, and the total procession requires some 4,000 cart-pullers. In the past, devotees would throw themselves under the wheels to be crushed under this moving building of the lord, giving rise to the English word "juggernaut". The carts are broken up for relics after the festival and are remade the following year.

The Kaaba, Mecca

Islam itself is conceived as a building, raised on five "pillars". The first four are profession of faith, prayer, almsgiving and fasting during the month of Ramadan. The fifth, which takes place in the month of Dhu-al-Hijjah, is pilgrimage (*hajj*) to Mecca in Saudi Arabia, the centre of the Islamic world, where Muhammad received God's word and law (later written down as the Koran). Every able-bodied Muslim man and woman should try to perform *hajj* at least once in a lifetime.

Mecca is the point of intersection between the vertical axis reaching up to heaven and the horizontal plane of human existence. For the *hajj*, pilgrims

stream to Mecca from all over the world; some journeys can take years and use up a lifetime's savings. Drawing near, pilgrims change into special clothing made of simple white sheets, symbolizing purity of soul and reducing all ranks to the same level. The pilgrims will re-enact, over several days, central events in the life of Muhammad.

The goal of the pilgrims, or *hajjis*, is the Great Mosque, al-Masjid al-Haram. In the centre of its vast courtyard, which is adorned at each corner by a pair of minarets, stands the massive black shrine called the Kaaba. Mecca was historically an oasis and trading town, and the Kaaba was originally a shrine to pre-Islamic deities. Muhammad's act of clearing out the idols in AD630 was a key moment in the development of Islamic monotheism.

ABOVE *A Hajj certificate from 1432, commemorating a pilgrim's visit to Mecca. Today, notably in West Africa,* hajjis *often paint pictures of the journey on an outer wall of their house.*

OPPOSITE, MAIN PICTURE *Hundreds of thousands of pilgrims crowd into the courtyard of the Great Mosque during the* hajj. *The Kaaba is a cubic building built of dark grey stone with a door seven feet (2.1 metres) above ground level on the east side. Framed in silver and inserted into the southeast corner of the building is a black stone, possibly a meteorite, said to have been received from the angel Gabriel. The exterior of the Kaaba is covered with a cloth, embroidered in gold and silver with a band of Koranic verses, which is renewed every year, while the interior is lined with marble and silver-gilt panels. On the first day, the pilgrim performs the* tawaf, *circumambulating the Kaaba seven times and attempting to kiss the black stone.*
OPPOSITE, LEFT *The Kaaba was built by Abraham (revered in Islam as a prophet) near the well of Zamzam, which was revealed to Abraham's wife Hagar by an angel. Leading out at an angle from the mosque, between the small hills of Safa and Marwah, is a wide covered walkway (top left of picture). Re-enacting Hagar's desperate search for water to save*

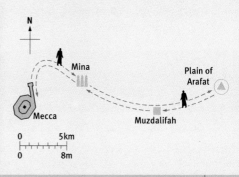

herself and her son Ishmael from dying of thirst in the desert, pilgrims run back and forth seven times along the walkway.

ABOVE RIGHT *From the Kaaba and the causeway, pilgrims proceed to the town of Mina and to the Plain of Arafat, where the Prophet gave his farewell sermon. Here he asked Allah if he had delivered Allah's message and fulfilled his calling, and in answer the crowd shouted, "Yes, by Allah you have!" Pilgrims return via Muzdalifah to Mina for three days, where they throw stones at three pillars representing Satan. In Mina a sheep, goat, camel or cow may be sacrificed, to commemorate Abraham's sacrifice of a lamb in place of his son. Lastly a final* tawaf *around the Kaaba is performed.*

Types and Traditions

Regional traditions of sacred architecture express in numerous ways what are believed to be eternal truths. In each culture, buildings reflect local ideas about the form of the cosmos, the nature of the gods, the way in which they dwell in the universe, and how ritual is performed.

At the same time, architects and craftspeople rely on an accumulation of experience, with the result that there is notable continuity in the buildings of diverse and even opposed theologies. The Greek temple was turned inside-out to create the Roman temple, which in turn added the dome. The early Christian basilica inherited the dome and passed it through Byzantium to the mosque, where it was further adapted to express the Islamic idea of Allah. Similar strands link the Hindu temple to Buddhist architecture throughout eastern Asia, or the evolution of building styles across Mesoamerica. In every region, incoming styles are modified by local religions and technologies. As theologies evolve, architecture gradually adapts existing models to express new ideas.

A view over the roofs of the old city of Jerusalem demonstrates both the diversity and the continuity of sacred architecture. Domes, spires and towers are built in the style characteristic of the region and show distinct architectural similarities, yet these forms represent mosques, churches and synagogues. The same basic structures of dome and cube are also visible in the domestic architecture of the city.

Megalithic monuments

Carnac in France is the site of more than 3,000 prehistoric stones. Possibly a lunar observatory, they were erected over the course of 5,000 years, and were once thought to be petrified Roman soldiers.

The word "megalith" means "huge stone". Megalithic cultures are, or have been, concentrated particularly in prehistoric western Europe, ancient Mesoamerica and present-day Southeast Asia and Oceania. The word generally describes very simple styles of building which use the shape of natural stone. But the term is also sometimes applied elsewhere when massive stones are used with more elaborate techniques of carving and dressing, as at some Olmec sites in Mexico and the early Inca site of Chavín in Peru. At the mysterious site of Tiahuanaco, 13,000 feet (4,000 metres) high in the Bolivian Andes, long lines of massive upright stones formed a continuous wall around a large square and an entrance was carved through a single block of stone to form the Gateway of the Sun.

In Europe, megalithic monuments from the Neolithic period (New Stone Age) are found mainly in Britain,

France, Spain, Portugal, Sardinia, Malta, southern Sweden and northern Germany. They were constructed at various times between the 5th and 2nd millennia BC. The most numerous type of monument is the burial chamber. This may take the form of passage-graves with a long entrance, such as Newgrange in Ireland; court-graves, named after their large semicircular entrance, found in Ireland and Sardinia; and dolmens, in which two or more upright stones support a horizontal slab. Another common type is the single standing stone or menhir ("long stone"). The largest and most spectacular megalithic monuments are the rows or circles composed of standing stones, common in Britain and northwestern France. At Stonehenge in southern England, the circle of standing stones was capped with lintels (see p.169).

Megalithic monuments were also widespread in ancient Southeast Asia and Oceania. In modern times they are particularly prominent in parts of tribal India, on the islands of Nias, Bali and Sumba in Indonesia, and in Polynesia. As in ancient Europe, they perform a range of functions. Among the Sora of India the shaman's assistants raise a menhir at each person's funeral, representing that person's continuing existence in the underworld (see pp.147). At the funeral of a chief in Nias or Sumba, massive stones of up to 30 tons are laid horizontally across dolmen supports. In modern Bali, as in ancient Polynesia, a row of menhirs wrapped in cloth is placed in an enclosed temple courtyard as a lodging for visiting ancestor spirits. Both cultures built rectangular stone pyramids, of which the largest in Polynesia – on Tahiti – had a base of 266 x 72 feet (81 x 22 metres). In Polynesia megaliths were also used as aids for navigation between tiny islands on the huge ocean. Sailors would study the sequence of stars as they came up against the stone. In Kiribati, nine stones on the shore point accurately toward three neighbouring islands, apparently showing the degree of drift associated with different currents.

WHY WERE THE ANCIENT MEGALITHS BUILT?

In the absence of written records, the interpretation of prehistoric monuments is often controversial. Stonehenge (see p.14), one of the largest and most mysterious stone circles, has been interpreted as a temple, meeting place, burial site, observatory and calendar, and may have been all of these. At the northeast of the site, an avenue leading from the centre gives an alignment to the midsummer sunrise, while an opening to the northwest is aligned to the midwinter setting of the moon.

The design of some tombs clearly links astronomy to rebirth. The passage-grave resembles a vagina leading into the womb and some tombs have entrances shaped very clearly like a vulva. This interpretation is borne out by the facing of the burial mound at Newgrange with white quartz, making the tomb resemble an egg. In many religions today the tomb is also a place of regeneration and rebirth, and it seems likely that this was also the case for many Neolithic peoples. At Newgrange at the winter solstice, the rays of the rising sun penetrate nearly 100 feet (30 metres) along the passage to the back wall. This was very carefully calculated, as the uphill gradient of the passage was compensated for by a tiny opening in a "roof box" which let in the sunlight. It is as if the deceased, just like the dying year, will be reborn at the touch of the returning sun.

The exterior of the burial mound at Newgrange in Ireland, built more than 5,000 years ago.

Avebury and Silbury Hill, England

NORTH SEA

IRELAND

UNITED KINGDOM

■ London

Avebury ● and Silbury Hill

ATLANTIC OCEAN

FRANCE

Avebury is a large Bronze Age structure in Wiltshire, built *c.*2600BC. An outer circle was made up of some 100 standing stones and was surrounded by a ditch and embankment nearly 1,400 feet (430 metres) across. To form this ditch, the chalk soil was scraped out with tools made from deer antlers. Inside, there were two smaller circles side by side, each of around 30 stones, and a cluster of larger stones in the middle. Today, only about a quarter of these stones remain between the cottages and gardens of the village that lies largely inside the outer circle.

The antiquarian William Stukeley drew and described the monument in the 18th century, shortly before much of it was destroyed to provide farming land and building materials. He identified two avenues of stones. One, still visible, leads from Avebury to a small stone circle on Overton Hill which has now disappeared. The other avenue (no longer visible) curved sinuously to the southwest. Stukeley called the avenues serpents and described Avebury as a serpent temple, shaped as an alchemical symbol of divine power, although this interpretation now seems doubtful.

Avebury is surrounded by the greatest concentration of large prehistoric monuments in Britain. Nearby are the West and East Kennet long barrows – passage-tombs dating from *c.*3600BC – and the massive Neolithic mound of Silbury Hill, whose true purpose or function remains a mystery.

OPPOSITE, MAIN PICTURE *Southwest of Avebury is Silbury Hill, at 130 feet (40 metres) high the largest artificial mound in Europe. It was once believed to be the burial mound of King Sil of local legend, but excavations have found a solid core of stone. The discovery of grass and flying ants inside shows that the hill was started in late July or early August, possibly c.2750–2660BC. It has inspired respect throughout history: even the Romans, building a straight military road, took a detour around Silbury Hill. Although excavations have failed to reveal its purpose, it has been speculated that it was an omphalos marking the navel of the world (see pp.142–3); the womb of a mother goddess; or a memorial to a chieftain.*
LEFT *The great circular enclosure of the Avebury monument is today bisected by the lines of roads, and the village has breached the outer ditch. Nonetheless the site retains an aura of ancient power. The conical mound of Silbury Hill rises out of the fields close by.*
OPPOSITE, BOTTOM LEFT *Part of the outer circle at Avebury. Twenty-seven stones are still standing out of the original 100 or so.*

RIGHT *The interior of West Kennet long barrow, a megalithic passage-grave near Avebury. A narrow passage, constructed of upright stones roofed with huge capstones, leads from the entrance of the tomb to the main chamber. It was built c.2500BC and used for burials for the next 1,000 years, after which the entrance was blocked with a massive stone.*

Egyptian temples

The Grand Approach to the Temple of Philae, by David Roberts (1796–1864). The huge entrance pylon dominates the complex, flanked by rows of lotus-topped columns.

As the river Nile retreated each year from the height of its flooding, it gradually revealed islands of mud. In the same way, according to Egyptian myth, a mound of dry land arose from the waters of Chaos, providing a place where the first god, Atum, could come into existence. Many temples were a representation in architecture of this primordial island: the visitor was drawn up steps or a ramp at every stage from the entrance through to the inner sanctum. The primeval mound, as the locus of creation, may also symbolize the potential for rebirth, an idea illustrated by the cenotaph of Sety I at Abydos, where the coffin was placed on an island surrounded by a channel of water.

The Egyptian temple was trabeate in construction, that is, made from upright posts and cross-beams. Roofs were simply flat lids. The wooden beams of the earliest temples were held up by stiff bundles of papyrus reeds, which symbolized the vegetation on the primordial island. Later, stone pillars continued to imitate these papyrus bundles, even down to the vertically ridged effect of the multiple stems. From the 3rd Dynasty onward, papyrus flowers were portrayed open and from the 5th Dynasty they were also shown in bud. Sometimes capitals portrayed the lotus (water-lily). The papyrus represented the delta area of Lower Egypt, the lotus Upper Egypt. These two species were often later combined in the same building to symbolize the unification of the two kingdoms.

The temple is essentially a long, straight, upward path, which in the most elaborate examples passes through an alternation of open, sun-drenched courts and the dark, cool interiors of gateways and halls and finally reaches the inner sanctum. The entrance to the temple was formed by a monumental gateway, or pylon, adorned with flags, multi-coloured carvings and colossal statues. The pillared hall, representing the island of mud, was like a forest of gigantic reeds and was often paved to resemble water; the ceiling was frequently painted with stars. The inner sanctum housed the statue of the god and was the god's dwelling-place, sometimes surrounded by other inner rooms containing model boats and priests' offices. As the path led toward the ultimate small enclosure, the ceilings became progressively lower, adding to the impression of depth and mystery.

During the course of some 3,000

The statues of the pharaoh Ramesses II outside his temple at Abu Simbel (13th century BC) were hewn out of the living rock. Although they are three-dimensional, the statues were still conceived to be viewed from the front.

years, a number of temples became enormous and complex. At Luxor and Karnak (see pp.90–91) the sense of a path was extended over centuries by adding a chain of further courts, each fronted by a pylon.

THE IMPORTANCE OF THE NILE

Egypt is a narrow strip of land on the banks of a long river, with desert beyond. The Blue Nile, bringing fertile silt from the mountains of Ethiopia, made Egyptian civilization possible. In ancient Egypt, the river rose rapidly from June to October, then fell gradually again. Agriculture was possible only from October, as the waters started to recede, and this left a great labour force available for monumental building during the flood period. The Nile was also the main avenue for transport – stone blocks of up to 15 tons were floated down it.

At Thebes in Upper Egypt, the "city of the dead" was built on the western bank; causeways led from the river to a necropolis of funerary temples and cliff tombs. Also on the west bank was the royal palace. The "city of the living", with settlements of workers' housing, lay on the eastern bank. The temple, with its long path, may also be modelled on the

The village of Beni Hasan is sited just above the former high-water mark, where the Nile flooded annually until the building of the Aswan High Dam in 1971. It is still possible to stand with one foot in the fields, the other in the desert.

Nile as a central axis with banks and fields on each side. The Egyptians may have conceived of space itself as long and narrow – an idea made physical in the shape of the temple.

The Temple of Amun at Karnak

Thebes was the capital of Egypt during the New Kingdom (*c.*1539–1075BC), and at its centre was the temple of the creator god Amun. The Temple of Amun was part of a vast temple complex at Karnak, the main treasury of a state rich with taxes and booty from the pharaohs' conquests.

The massive pylon, or gateway, at the entrance is the first of a procession of six, as the path leads through the first open courtyard to the second pylon, with two statues of Ramesses II (1279–1213BC) in front. This pylon leads to the hypostyle hall, with its colonnades of huge columns. The great hall, which would have been roofed, gives the impression of being a passageway rather than a chamber, a stage on the journey through the temple. This feeling is highlighted by the two rows of huge columns that form the central path, in contrast to the smaller columns beyond, which are out of alignment with the large columns. The space on either side of the path was dim and fragmented by the staggered pillars, while the central path was higher, sharply defined, and lit from window-slits just below the roof.

The path leads on through a succession of darker inner halls, via three more pylons, some originally with gold doors and silver floors, to the sanctum of the sun god, built by Thutmose I (1493–1482BC). This chamber, the focus of the whole temple, contained a statue of Amun in a shrine of gold and gems.

ABOVE *Priests ritually purified themselves in the temple's sacred lake. The obelisks, quarried from Aswan, are inscribed with hieroglyphs.*
RIGHT *A 19th-century painting of the hypostyle hall by David Roberts. The columns – 70 feet (21 metres) high, 12 feet (3.6 metres) across – are decorated with reliefs of the pharaoh's triumphs and capped with carved papyrus flowers.*

ABOVE *An avenue of ram-headed sphinxes leads up to the first great entrance pylon; the ram was a symbol of Amun.*

BELOW *Pillars were carved in the shape of reeds and lotus or papyrus blossoms or buds, evoking the creation myth, in which a primordial island remained after flood waters had receded (see pp.88–9); according to a widely held view, the whole temple embodies this myth.*

RIGHT *Passing along the avenue of sphinxes (A) and through the first pylon, visitors find themselves in a vast sunlit courtyard, a contrast to the shadowy hypostyle hall (B) into which the second pylon leads. Via further pylons, halls and courtyards, the inner sanctum (C) is reached, where only the pharaoh and his priests were allowed. Originally, a gold and gem-encrusted shrine contained a statue of Amun, although today this is lost. The god was believed to reside in his statue, and he was*

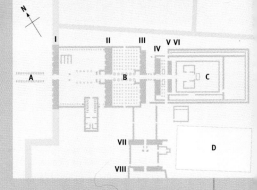

tended by shaven-headed priests who ritually washed him, fed him and dressed him in fine linen three times a day. In the grounds is the sacred lake (D), which was used by the priests to purify themselves before carrying out their rituals. The temple was extended by successive pharaohs from the inner sanctum outward (the roman numerals on the plan indicate pylons).

Shinto shrines and temples

The Japanese religion Shinto (Way of the Gods) emerged from ancient folk ideas of dynamic divinity manifest in all things, animate and inanimate. There are believed to be an infinite number of deities, or *kami*, and these may reside in great people, in ancestors, in trees, mountains, rocks, waterfalls and other features of the environment as well as in phenomena such as birth and decay. Because of this concept of nature as permeated with divinity, Shinto shrines are often found at places of natural beauty or sites with an air of grandeur or mystery about them; shrines themselves are often places for the worship of nature. Concomitant with this perspective is a respect for the architectural use of natural materials in the building of shrines.

Kyushu Temple, Japan. The rope over the posts is reminiscent of the first simple toriis *(gateways), and the strips of white paper (*gohei*) symbolize the presence of the* kami *(gods).*

Four prototypical shapes are found in Shinto shrines, according to the historian Nitschke: the pillar, the hut, the mountain and the funnel. Most shrines contain more than one of these elements. All are essentially movable and renewable, reflecting the idea that the shrine is the temporary abode (*yorishiro*) of a deity who periodically visits the people. All four models derive from the notion of the archetypal bundle of grass (*shime*) tied together with the sacred straw rope, which was originally used in ancient times to signify occupation or ownership of land. In the course of time, such marks of the humanization of the world were sacralized.

As Shinto evolved, so did its shrines. The very early, simple, outdoor altars had become temples by the 7th century AD, their style bearing an architectural resemblance to older raised-floor wooden dwellings and rice-stores. From around the same time, after the introduction of Buddhism to Japan, Shinto temples also imitated the distinctive style of Chinese Buddhist temples. In a departure from the simple early style, these were brightly coloured and elaborately ornamented.

Modern shrines are built in a diversity of styles, but most are situated within a garden or amid trees, reflecting the significance of nature, and most have a similar layout. At the entrance is a gateway, or *torii*. This originally consisted of two posts set in the ground with a straw rope stretched between them; the rope was later replaced by a wooden crosspiece extending past the posts and a second crosspiece just below, connecting the posts. Eventually

PORTABLE SHRINES AND RITUAL FLOATS

In Shinto belief, gods only temporarily come down into shrines and natural objects. Just as the god is mobile, so too is its humanly constructed vessel. This often takes the form of a float – a "mountain" marking the descent of a deity. Floats used in the 1,100-year-old Gion Festival of Kyoto consist of a wonderful variety of square, four-wheeled chariots, sometimes with a small roofed shrine for the

*A portable shrine (*mikoshi*) is carried at the Sanja Matsuri festival in Tokyo.*

deity, sometimes with a hemispherical mound representing the mountain.

Most ritual floats are topped with pine or cedar branches. The spiky leaves act as a conduit for a deity residing in the "high plain of heaven", who is called down to the summit of a "divinely selected fire mountain", then guided down to the festival site via the branches of the tree. The floats have evolved and diversified over the centuries; many signify mountains without now bearing any visual resemblance to them.

---

the *torii* became an elaborate architectural form in its own right – sometimes it stands alone in the landscape, denoting a sacred place such as a mountain to which it may lead.

Passing through a *torii*, the devotee crosses the threshold separating the secular from the sacred world, and enters the precinct of the shrine. There, preparing to enter the presence of the gods, the worshipper cleanses him- or herself with a scoop of pure water from a stone trough. The shrine itself will typically consist of one or more halls, and an inner sanctuary – the domain of the priest – containing the image of the *kami*. Some shrines are very small; others are great temple complexes dedi-

Devotees at the Kasuga shrine in Nara. In Shinto, worshippers ring a bell or clap to signal to the kami *the beginning and end of a prayer.*

cated to several Shinto deities, and contain many subsidiary buildings in their precincts, including stalls where good-luck charms are sold, later to be hung up for the attention of the *kami*.

Just as a god comes down to a shrine, it can also go away. In modern Japan, where city-dwellers may find it difficult to climb up to high mountain shrines or where sacred sites have been razed for development, Shinto priests may have to move gods to new locations. This is done by ritually returning the god, temporarily, to its original home on a far peak, while the rocks used as its shrine-vessel are wrapped in white cloth. Only in that wrapped and empty state can the rocks be moved to their new site.

The Ise Grand Shrine, Japan

SEA OF JAPAN

SOUTH KOREA

JAPAN

Tokyo ■

● Ise

PACIFIC OCEAN

The Grand Shrine at Ise is the most sacred shrine in Japan, dating back to the 3rd or 4th century AD. In a ritual that first took place in the 8th century, the buildings that comprise the Grand Shrine are destroyed every 20 years and new ones are built on a carefully prepared adjacent site. The new shrines, although identical to the old ones, are not considered a replica of Ise, but are Ise re-created afresh. The process reveals the Shinto understanding of nature as constantly renewed. The shrines were last rebuilt in 1993.

Set amid ancient and lofty *Cryptomeria* trees, the Grand Shrine consists of two similar complexes about four miles (six kilometres) apart, dedicated to two major goddesses. Naiku, the Inner Shrine and the holiest part of the entire complex, is dedicated to the sun goddess Amaterasu Omikami. She is the *kami* from whom the imperial family is believed to descend, and only the emperor, his family and his priests may enter the precinct. The Outer Shrine, or Geku, is dedicated to Toyouke no Omikami, the rice goddess.

The shrines express the Shinto spiritual ideals of purity and simplicity. The buildings are raised on posts about seven feet (two metres) above the ground, in a style that may have been based on the raised-floor dwellings of ancient Japan. The buildings are made from the wood of the *hinoki* tree, a species of white cypress, which is planed smooth and then left in its natural state.

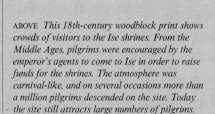

ABOVE *This 18th-century woodblock print shows crowds of visitors to the Ise shrines. From the Middle Ages, pilgrims were encouraged by the emperor's agents to come to Ise in order to raise funds for the shrines. The atmosphere was carnival-like, and on several occasions more than a million pilgrims descended on the site. Today the site still attracts large numbers of pilgrims.*

ABOVE *The entrance to Naiku, the Inner Shrine, at Ise. Only members of the emperor's household may pass beyond this threshold. Naiku contains the sacred mirror, symbol of the sun goddess Amaterasu, which in Shinto myth was brought to earth by her grandson Honinigi, and which is one of the symbols that serve to legitimate the divine rule of the emperor.*

MAIN PICTURE, TOP *An arched footbridge spans the Isuzu River which the visitor must cross in order to approach the Inner Shrine. First, he or she passes through a simple* torii *(gateway), thus stepping from profane into sacred space.*
ABOVE LEFT *Harmony of structure is evident everywhere in Ise's buildings of wood and thatch, which, being torn down and reconstructed every*

20 years, are at the same time ancient and new.
ABOVE *A detail from the roof of one of the shrine buildings. The roofs have to shed Japan's heavy rainfall and they are thatched in a delicate curve from strips of* hinoki *(Japanese cypress) bark and then trimmed. The cross-shaped end beams and the vertical pillar reflect the archetypal forms of ancient Japanese architecture.*

Mosques

According to Islam, Allah is everywhere, and so the mosque is a prayer-hall rather than a building enshrining a deity. The interior of the prayer-hall is an expression in architecture of *tawhid*, the doctrine of divine unity. The mosque focuses, not on mass or surface, but on space. Once inside the prayer-hall there is no path and the devotee is encouraged to linger and contemplate this open, undivided space.

The earliest mosques were based on the Prophet Muhammad's house in Medina. Later, each region developed its own style, usually keeping the early distinction between an outer courtyard and an inner sanctuary or prayer-hall. In India the mosque was influenced by the Hindu temple. In the eastern Mediterranean the influence of the Byzantine church can be seen – for example, in the 17th-century Blue Mosque in Istanbul (see also p.166), which consists of a square hall with a minimum of internal supports, covered with a dome and surrounded by a porch and minarets. In a typical mosque the prayer-hall is entered only after washing at a tap or a fountain outside, and in some courtyards the fountain becomes a major architectural feature in its own right.

Muhammad had sent his followers to the rooftops to call the faithful to prayer, and the minaret soon developed as a special tower, from which the muezzin (crier) proclaims the hours of prayer five times a day. In Syria and North Africa, minarets are square with several stories. In Iraq they are wide and spiral, in Iran and Turkey slim and cylindrical supporting high balconies.

The Arabic word for mosque, *masjid*, means a place where one prostrates one-

The Mosque of Sultan Ahmet, or Blue Mosque (1606–19), in Istanbul, has typical slender Turkish minarets.

self in obedience to the law of Allah, and the meaning of the word "Islam" refers to the sense of peace that comes from obedience and submission to this law. The sacred geography of Islam reaches from within the bounds of the mosque to encompass the whole world. Set into an inside wall of the prayer-hall is a niche called the *mihrab*, which is always oriented toward Mecca (see pp.80–81) – the *qiblah* (centre) of the Islamic universe. Thus in Britain, Algeria or Canada, it will be oriented to the east or southeast, while in India, Indonesia or Australia it will face the west or northwest.

The *mihrab* is often lavishly decorated and hung about with lights, and may also be surmounted by a dome – a symbol of paradise. It unites each congregation within its own local mosque and orients all worshippers toward the centre of the Islamic faith. Five times a day, congregations line up facing this niche behind the prayer-leader (imam) to pray to Allah. Women pray in a separate area from men, and where a congregation is all-female, it is led by a female imam. In large collective mosques, known as Friday (*jami*) mosques, the congregation also listens on Fridays and holidays (*id*) to sermons from the raised pulpit (*minbar*) built alongside the *mihrab*.

Islam's reverence for the written word also made the mosque a centre of literacy, and the building is often accompanied by an Islamic school (*madrase*). The ritual of prayer is the foundation for a way of life, so that religious leaders originally also used the mosque as the place from which to govern the community and administer the law.

The mosque contains no visual representation of Allah or of the human form – no statues or pictures. Instead, surfaces are covered with an elaborate geometrical ornamentation based on vibrant patterns of straight or flowing lines, passing over and under each other in a restless rhythm of vegetation and arabesques. The doctrine of *tawhid* teaches that Allah is both the source and the culmination of all diversity, and patterns may also incorporate the Arabic letters for his name (see p.49). Allah himself is conceived as light, and the perforated grilles and pierced screens set into mosque walls serve to blur the distinction between light and solid substance.

"ANTHILL" MOSQUES

In much of West Africa, village mosques are often made of mud on a framework of sticks, supported by heavy buttresses. The pinnacles may be an enlarged form of the ancestral pillars placed at the entrance of many local house compounds, and the entire mosque may also be an imitation of the large termite hills that are found throughout the region. Like a termite hill, the mud mosque needs frequent repair, and the sticks serve as a permanent scaffolding. Because of the limitations of the building material, the interior is small and dark. Larger mosques in the towns, despite being made of cement, often reproduce this shape.

A white-painted "anthill" mosque in northern Ghana, lacking the dome and minarets that are typical of mosques in the Middle East and Central Africa.

Isfahan, Iran

In a bowl formed by arid mountains in present-day Iran rises an elaborately planned city of mosques, palaces and pavilions, the high point of 17th-century Persian art and architecture. The garden city of Isfahan, celebrated by Persian poets as "half the world", was laid out by Shah Abbas, ruler of an empire with trading relations stretching from China to Sweden.

In the huge Maidan-i-Shah (Shah's Square), he built two contrasting mosques faced with light-reflecting glazed tiles in shades of turquoise, cobalt and lapis lazuli. Due to the need to orient the *mihrab* toward Mecca, the mosques are not aligned with the square outside and are entered through an ingenious, bent "elbow" corridor.

The Sheikh Lutfullah Mosque was built *c*.1603–17 and named after the Shah's father-in-law, a great Islamic scholar. It is small, with a single prayer-hall and no courtyard. The exquisite dome is slightly flattened, echoing an earlier Seljuk style, with plant tendrils, evoking the Islamic paradise, picked out in black outline on a background that according to the light seems beige or pink. But this mosque was too modest for the growing splendour of the Shah's court, and in 1611 he began to build the Masjid-i-Shah (Shah's Mosque) with its striking blue dome. The gateway functioned both to close off the south side of the square and to emphasize the Shah's power. The mosque was completed in 1638, nine years after the Shah's death.

ABOVE *The interior of the Lutfullah Mosque: the* mihrab *is set into the left wall, facing Mecca. The floor is of shimmering blue tiles.*
LEFT *One of the minarets of the Shah's Mosque, and the slightly pointed turquoise dome, covered in twining, tendril-like decoration. At the base of the dome sacred texts are written in white Arabic calligraphy against a band of darker blue.*

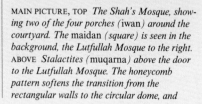

MAIN PICTURE, TOP *The Shah's Mosque, showing two of the four porches (*iwan*) around the courtyard. The* maidan *(square) is seen in the background, the Lutfullah Mosque to the right.*
ABOVE *Stalactites (*muqarna*) above the door to the Lutfullah Mosque. The honeycomb pattern softens the transition from the rectangular walls to the circular dome, and* symbolizes the crystallization of celestial ether into earthly form.*
ABOVE *The interior of the dome in the Lutfullah Mosque. The pattern, with its mesmerizing quality, has been seen as representing the descent of the divine, showing the movement from the unity of God at the centre to the multiplicity of his creation around the edges.*

Hindu temples

The Hindu temple is essentially a house for the deity (*deva-sthanam*), and it usually has an inner sanctum where the god's image is kept (see p.27). The deity is believed to be present in this image. The temple reproduces the form of the Hindu cosmos through a *mandala* (cosmic diagram; see pp.12–13, 36–7) which is used as its ground-plan.

Hinduism is not a single unified religion but combines numerous spiritual traditions, elements of which are also found in distinct religions such as Buddhism and Jainism. In all these religions the temples and forms of worship

At the 13th-century Sun Temple at Konarak, Orissa, thick walls enclose a central sanctum. The temple is covered with carvings of, among other subjects, mythological characters and erotic figures.

have continually influenced each other. The earliest surviving Hindu shrines, the temples of Udayagiri in Orissa, are hewn entirely out of the living rock, in imitation of Buddhist models. Such cave-temples embody the idea of an inner sanctum, the *garbhagriha* (womb-house). Later, free-standing temples opened out the sanctum in the four cardinal directions by adding projecting alcoves to the exterior to house representations of deities.

The classic form of the great Hindu temple developed during the Middle Ages (*c*.500–1500), during the same period that the great cathedrals were built in Europe. Beneath numerous elaborations and additions, these follow the same basic structure as the early temples. The womb-house contains a central sanctum (*vimana*) where the main statue or image of the god is enshrined. Directly above this sanctum rises a tower (*shikhara*) representing Mount Meru as the centre of the universe (see pp.22–3). The temple is surrounded by a path or veranda for circumambulation (see p.78), and there is usually an adjoining assembly-hall (*mandapa*).

The *shikhara* is generally built up out of repetitions of the same shape or motif, as if it were constructed out of repeating cells. The surface of the temple gives the effect of concentrated devotional ornamentation, being often entirely covered with carvings of deities, mythical figures and heroes from the Hindu epics.

There are two main traditions of the Hindu temple – the Nagara (northern)

WAYSIDE SHRINES

In every village and city of India there are wayside shrines which serve local concerns. At a corner of a bustling street, under a spreading tree in the fields, or beside a road in the hills, such shrines usually consist of a platform on which are placed images of spirits, ancestors and heroes. It is impossible to decipher the iconography of wayside shrines without knowing local legends, as a deity may take several forms. Dev Narayan, worshipped in Rajasthan as an incarnation of the god Vishnu or Krishna, appears variously as a hero on a horse, or as a rearing hooded snake, or in the abstract form of five bricks.

People set up shrines for protection against various ills, such as infertility, disease, snake-bites, the evil eye, or punishment by neglected

A woman makes an offering at a small wayside shrine. Offerings may be made to forestall misfortune caused by malicious gods, or for specific purposes such as the cure of an illness.

ancestors. Powerful goddesses and fierce gods of the boundaries are also common. The shrines, being open to anyone irrespective of sex, caste or religion, reflect this diversity.

The wayside shrine is a concept that spreads beyond architectural structures. It may be a worshipped tree, or a mobile form such as a scroll or a cupboard shrine taken from place to place to accompany a recounting of legends. It may even be alive – a mendicant accepted as an embodiment of a god becomes a "human shrine".

and the Dravida (southern). The northern tradition is notable for its development of the image of the ribbed seed of a medicinal plant, *amala*, symbolizing fertility, health and fruitful life-processes. Originally used to top the head of the free-standing pillar, this seed, in greatly expanded style, came to provide the main roof-form of the temple, surmounting its central axis. Other towers and shrines were grouped below it, providing architectural support for this image of fertility and the eternal cycles of life. In the southern tradition the primary form is a pillared pavilion with barrel-roof. Small pavilions cluster round a taller one, forming the tiers of a pyramidal structure.

Communal services and festivals take place in Hindu temples on auspicious dates, but worshippers may also enter to make offerings at any time. The deities on the exterior are protectors of the locality and are more accessible than those inside. The building demarcates ever more sacred space, culminating in the sanctum, often behind doors or a grille. Here the worshippers make their offerings of flowers, rice, fruit or sweets, and the priest hands back some of these offerings as *prasad*, the blessing of the god in the form of his leftover food.

Madurai, India

The 17th-century Minakshi Temple at Madurai in Tamil Nadu does more than merely accommodate the god's shrine and priests. Like many other temples in southern India, it provides for both individual and community worship, with complex groupings of sanctums and courtyards. These are linked by nine magnificent tower gateways (*gopuram*), which become smaller as they near the central shrines. Their surfaces teem with colourful statues of deities and mythological figures.

The Minakshi Temple is dedicated to Shiva (in his local incarnation, Sundareshwarar) and his consort Minakshi – it is she who, unusually, is the presiding deity. A sculpture celebrating their divine marriage stands outside the Sundareshwarar shrine. The temple compound is surrounded by an outer wall with four massive, nine-storied *gopurams*. Inside, the temple has long corridors and roofed quadrangles, supported by some 2,000 carved columns and decorated with murals depicting episodes from the lives of the gods.

Pilgrims wind their way along processional paths, past images of great heroes from the Hindu epic, the *Mahabharata*, halting frequently to make offerings to minor deities. The progression toward the innermost sanctum is measured by the length of the passages, which seems to be exaggerated by the countless turns made on the way. Before entering the inner shrines, devotees must ritually bathe in the sacred Golden Lotus tank.

ABOVE *The Golden Lotus tank, where it is said that the god Indra gathered flowers to offer to Shiva. Pilgrims bathe in the tank to purify themselves before entering the inner sanctum.*
ABOVE RIGHT *One of the long corridors in the Minakshi temple. The pillars are ornamented with a variety of carved subjects, including lions, galloping horses, deities and mythical creatures.*

OPPOSITE, MAIN PICTURE *A view of the Minakshi Temple showing the gopurams. It has been estimated that there are more than 30 million carvings on these gateways. The larger gopurams indicate the external boundary of the temple, while the smaller ones are inside the compound. The golden cupola is the central shrine toward which all worshippers penetrate.*

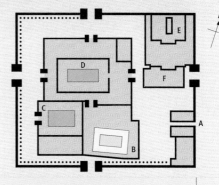

ABOVE *The outer circle of the Minakshi Temple is filled with a tremendous sense of life, bustle and energy, perhaps more reminiscent of a market than of a temple. This is where pilgrims buy the offerings for use in their* puja *(worship) in the deeper, more sacred areas of the temple.* Puja *items include coconuts, ghee (clarified butter), flower garlands, milk and incense.*

ABOVE *A simplified plan of the temple showing its principal elements: (A) the main entrance; (B) the Golden Lotus tank; (C) the Minakshi shrine; (D) the Shiva shrine; (E) the hall of the thousand pillars; (F) the pavilion of Nandi (Shiva's mount, the bull). The nine* gopurams *in the outer walls and leading to the inner shrines are shown in heavy black.*

Buddhist temples

The historical Buddha, Siddhartha Gautama, lived in north India in the 6th century BC, and it was there that Buddhism first took root. After his death, the religion spread throughout Asia, adapting to new conditions and giving rise to a huge diversity of Buddhist art and architecture. The first groups of monks congregated around the domed *stupas* containing relics of the Buddha (see box). Later, *chaityas* (temples or assembly-halls) and *viharas* (monasteries) were constructed alongside.

The temple is the main Buddhist sanctuary, in which the laity attend services and make offerings. It is often part of a larger complex such as a monastery,

where monks concentrate on meditation and self-enlightenment. An important part of Buddhist doctrine is generosity or the giving of *dana* (donations) with which the donor accrues the spiritual merit that leads to ever better births in the cycle of reincarnation. Temples contain an altar where devotees make offerings of food, incense or flowers, often accompanied by chanting and prayer.

Many temples are built on a *mandala* plan (cosmic diagram, see pp.12–13), so that the Buddhist cosmos is mapped out by the building. For example, at Angkor Thom in Cambodia, the tall central temple represents Mount Meru, the cosmic axis, while a surrounding moat recalled the primordial ocean.

A Buddhist temple usually contains a wealth of images, for both worship and instruction. Many ancient temples, such as Ajaṅta in India and Dun Huang in China, were caves hewn out of rock, containing large carvings of the Buddha or murals depicting scenes from his life. In the Theravada tradition (the conservative southern school of Buddhism) the statues and paintings are of the Buddha in conventional postures – typically teaching, meditating or reclining. Devotees recognize these as stages on the Buddha's path to *nirvana* (enlightenment). The more devotional of the two major traditions, Mahayana, emphasizes *bodhisattvas*, enlightened beings who strive to lead others to *nirvana*. Mahayana temples contain images of such figures, together with a pantheon of saints and benign or fierce deities.

The 14th–15th-century Shwe Dagon pagoda in Rangoon, Myanmar (Burma), is dominated by a gilded stupa *and incorporates many smaller shrines – their spires are unique to the region.*

THE *STUPA*

The dome-shaped *stupa* is the primary Buddhist monument. Deriving from ancient kingly funeral mounds, the *stupa* was adopted by Buddhists as a reliquary (relic container). After the Buddha died and had been cremated (according to legend, leaving no ashes), any remains were divided up between ten places, and a consecrated mound or *stupa* was erected over each relic. Later, *stupas* constructed for the relics of other holy figures such as monks and saints.

The *stupa* embodies a complex symbolism. Intimately linked to the death of the Buddha, it is the ultimate monument to his *parinirvana* – his final transcendence. The dome represents *nirvana* (enlightenment, liberation from worldly desire and suffering), and is also a symbolic mountain (see pp.22–3). The pole or spire on top of the dome refers to, as well as the cosmic axis, the *bodhi* tree under which the Buddha attained enlightenment, and therefore signifies the Buddha's compassion. The square base represents moral restraint.

The cult of the *stupa* began to proliferate in the 3rd century BC, under the Buddhist emperor Ashoka. Many were covered with carvings of significant events in the Buddha's life and previous lives, although the very early *stupas* depicted his presence only in symbolic form (a wheel, a *bodhi* tree, a miniature *stupa*).

The *stupa* has varying features. In Nepal some *stupas*, such as Svayambhunath in Kathmandu, have a unique 13-tiered steeple surmounting the dome, representing the 13 Buddhist heavens, and a gilded square base, on each side of which is a pair of huge eyes, possibly representing the all-seeing Buddha. At Pagan in Myanmar (Burma), bell- or drum-shaped *stupas* form part of *cetiya* (*chaitya*) temples, with a stepped pyramidal base and a spire. In Thailand, the *stupa* is often shaped like a lotus-bud and topped with a gold finial.

The Sri Lankan *stupa* (*dagoba*), breast-shaped and painted white, is associated locally with mother's milk. The Singhalese for relic, *dhatu*, is also the word for semen. The *stupa* therefore represents regenerative power through both male and female imagery.

The Great Stupa at Sanchi, India (3rd century BC), was built by the emperor Ashoka, who converted to Buddhism after the carnage of a battle led him to understand the Buddha's teaching on suffering.

Wat Arun, Bangkok

Until the mid-13th century, Thailand was dominated by the Hindu Khmers, and although Buddhism gained the ascendancy, much Thai architecture reflects the influence of its Khmer antecedents. Brick and wood replaced much of the Khmer stone, reflecting the Buddhist concern with the impermanence of matter and also giving their temples the light, fairytale effect for which it is famous. While Wat Arun (Temple of the Dawn), on the Chao Phraya River, was completed in the mid-19th century, it is an elegant example of the Khmer temple style that was adopted in the Ayutthaya period (1350–1767).

At its centre is a *prang* – a tall, tower-like monument, rounded at the top, containing niches that hold relics or images of the Buddha or holy men. The *prang* represents the 33 heavens or 33 stages that must be lived through in order to reach perfection; its shape is also an allusion to Mount Meru, the cosmic axis. At Wat Arun, a steep stairway climbs each side of the tower at the cardinal points. Three terraces, representing the three worlds of Buddhist cosmology, allow circumambulation at each level. At the corners of the temple complex are four smaller *prangs* with niches containing statues of the god of the wind. With its tall central tower and many-coloured decoration, the temple has attracted the patronage of the divine royal lineage, and Wat Arun has become a symbol of Thailand itself.

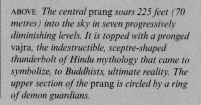

ABOVE *The central* prang *soars 225 feet (70 metres) into the sky in seven progressively diminishing levels. It is topped with a pronged* vajra, *the indestructible, sceptre-shaped thunderbolt of Hindu mythology that came to symbolize, to Buddhists, ultimate reality. The upper section of the* prang *is circled by a ring of demon guardians.*

ABOVE *The surface of Wat Arun is decorated throughout with multi-coloured ceramics – pieces of broken Chinese tiles that were donated by devotees – evoking the mythical world of Mount Meru. Such elaborate decoration has its basis in the Hindu (Khmer) belief that the elements of the temple should be a reflection of the beauties of heaven.*

ABOVE *The temple complex of Wat Arun is situated on the banks of the Chao Phraya River, partly because Thai Buddhist architectural convention has it that the* viharn *(or* vihara, *the worship- or assembly-hall) of the monks should face water. This is not only an echo of the primordial ocean encircling Mount Meru but also a reflection of the fact that the* bodhi *tree, beneath which the Buddha sat when he achieved enlightenment, faced a river.*

Surrounding the monks' assembly-hall (not seen) is a colonnaded cloister lined with a row of gilded statues of the Buddha four feet (1.5 metres) tall; this cloister is designed as a tranquil place of meditation for the monks. To the west of the main tower is a prasad, *an elegant hall traditionally reserved – here as at many other Thai temples – for worship by the Thai royal family.*

RIGHT *At the foot of each of the stairways is a* mandapa *(porch or pavilion). Each contains an image portraying an important event in the life of the Buddha – his birth; a scene of meditation; the Buddha preaching; and his death.*

Synagogues and the Temple of Solomon

The Temple, the House of God, was built in stone by King Solomon in Jerusalem in the 10th century BC, on the site where the Hebrew patriarch Abraham had gone to sacrifice his son Isaac. A main hall led to an inner sanctum containing the Ark of the Covenant. Rites were conducted by hereditary priests called *kohen* and, as with other types of temple in the ancient Near East and Mediterranean, ordinary worshippers remained outside, by the altar from which burnt offerings were sent up to God.

Two Orthodox Jewish men pray at the Wailing Wall in Jerusalem, all that remains of the original Temple.

The Temple was the centre of Jewish religious life. After its destruction by the Babylonians in 586BC it was rebuilt, but was finally destroyed by the Romans in AD70. One wall remains – the so-called "Wailing Wall" of the Jews. In AD691 the site of the Temple Mount became the Muslim shrine of the Dome of the Rock (see p.141).

The synagogue ("assembly") is based on a very different concept, and became widespread only after the final destruction of the Temple, as part of a democratic movement founded on rabbis ("teachers") rather than *kohens*. The synagogue is not a consecrated building, since God does not reside there as he did in the Temple. A living-room or even a hired cinema can serve as a synagogue. Permanent buildings often are not very formally structured, and loosely follow the style of the local Christian or Muslim majority. A rabbinical school (*midrash*) may be attached to the building, as one of the main roles of the synagogue is the study of the Talmud (Jewish law and legend). Orthodox synagogues incorporate a separate room or gallery in which women are segregated, although this feature was abolished by the 19th-century Jewish Reform movement in their synagogues. The Reformers also introduced the organ into their

The style of La Ghriba synagogue at Djerba, Tunisia, with its Arabic-type arches and mosaics, is clearly influenced by local Islamic architecture.

DURA-EUROPOS

The synagogue that was excavated in 1932 at Dura-Europos, a Roman fortress in Syria, challenged assumptions about early Judaism and revealed how much the synagogue has changed since AD245. The inside walls are covered with paintings. It is clear that the rabbis had not yet standardized Judaism, that representations of the human figure were used freely, and that Jewish paintings of Bible stories may have strongly influenced early Christian art. A nearby building, also excavated, was a Christian house-church.

The paintings at Dura-Europos include images of animals and theatrical masks as well as episodes from the Bible.

synagogues, in addition to the traditional unaccompanied singing.

The focus of ritual in all synagogues is the Ark, a cabinet containing the scrolls of the Torah (the first five books of the Bible given by God to Moses on Mount Sinai). The Torah is often richly ornamented in silver, but is not an object of worship. It is venerated because it contains the word of God, who is the only true object of worship. This is reflected in the synagogue's orientation, the Ark being set into the wall facing the Temple Mount in Jerusalem. Near the Ark is a platform or pulpit (*bimah*) from which portions of the Torah are chanted.

As in Islam, God (Yahweh) may not be portrayed – a prohibition that served in biblical times to highlight the contrast with neighbouring idolatrous tribes. The decoration in a synagogue is often abstract, with geometric designs and Hebrew calligraphy.

Many medieval synagogues in Europe have been either destroyed or converted into churches. Important synagogues have survived in Prague, Amsterdam, Toledo, Cracow, Regensburg and Budapest; the 12th-century synagogue at Worms in Germany, destroyed by the Nazis, has been faithfully reconstructed.

The transition from Temple worship to synagogue assembly was directly linked to a change in the use of architecture. Communication with God through animal sacrifice in the Temple courtyard was replaced by an emphasis on righteous actions before the Torah inside the synagogue. But the Temple remains a powerful symbol and serves by its very absence as a focus for a Jewish sense of longing and exile. The liturgy in the Orthodox synagogue still looks forward to the time when the Messiah will return, the Temple will be rebuilt and its ritual will begin again.

Beth Sholom, Pennsylvania

Beth Sholom ● Philadelphia

UNITED STATES
OF AMERICA

ATLANTIC
OCEAN

The synagogue of Beth Sholom, in a suburb of Philadelphia, was dedicated in 1959, the result of a fertile collaboration between the architect Frank Lloyd Wright (who died the same year) and the then Rabbi of Beth Sholom, Mortimer Cohen.

Every aspect of the building has intrinsic religious significance, so that meaning is embedded in its very fabric. Designed to represent Mount Sinai, the site where Jewish holy law was revealed by God to Moses, the synagogue is built in the shape of a pyramidal mountain. God appeared to Moses in the form of light, and Beth Sholom seems almost an embodiment of light. Its walls and roof are of white glass and cream fibreglass, so that during the day the interior is illuminated by a constantly changing light, and at night the building shines out like a flaming Mount Sinai. Along the three steel girders (signifying the three Hebrew patriarchs) from which the roof is suspended are seven stylized *menorahs* (seven-branched candelabra).

In the vast main sanctuary, the absence of internal supports allows for an airy and unobstructed space, its egalitarian nature emphasized by the fact that the 1,020 seats are arranged around the Ark rather than in conventional rows. The hall is dominated by the 40-foot (12-metre) concrete monolith representing the Tablets of the Law. In front of the monolith stands the black walnut Ark, which contains ten scrolls of the Torah.

ABOVE *The coloured glass of the central chandelier symbolizes the different colours through which, in the Jewish mystic tradition (Kabbala), God is thought to reveal himself.*
LEFT *Above the Ark is a glass and aluminium ornament, the "Wings", containing the eternal light symbolic of God's presence; the Hebrew word for "holy" is set above the whole monolith.*

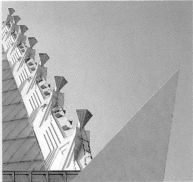

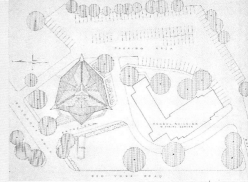

MAIN PICTURE, TOP *In front of the building is a pool, a symbol of purity recalling the laver (basin for ritual washing) outside the Temple. The entrance canopy symbolizes the joined hands of the priest outstretched in blessing.*
ABOVE *The prominent stylized* menorahs *(seven-branched candelabra) along the girders are visible from any point around the building.*

ABOVE *One of Frank Lloyd Wright's original plans for Beth Sholom. The distorted hexagon shape symbolizes the cupped hands of a priest, the two side projections the priest's thumbs. Walking into a sacred building, Wright said, should feel like "resting in the very hands of God", and the architectural features of his synagogue combine to convey this effect.*

Mesoamerican temples

For well over 2,000 years, until the Spanish destruction of the Aztec capital Tenochtitlán in 1525, the general form and setting of Mesoamerican temples remained unchanged. The temple stood on a platform at the top of a high pyramid, which rose in a number of terraces or stages. At the foot of the pyramid lay a sacrificial altar, a plaza and other open spaces such as ball courts.

The pyramid was usually square or rectangular, and the temple was approached up one or more sides of the pyramid by a centrally positioned monumental flight of stairs. Originally these stairs were set into the mass of the pyramid, but later they came to stand out and were elaborately ornamented. The grand staircases were used mainly by priests, while the congregation gathered below around the altar where most sacrifices were performed. A few pyramids had an additional altar in front of the temple at the top.

The main pyramid in the Aztec capital of Tenochtitlán was the Templo Mayor (Great Temple; see also p.64). The platform at the top of the pyramid supported twin temples, each representing a mountain. One temple was dedi-

A FOREST OF WORLD TREES

Whereas the pyramids built by the Toltec and Aztec civilizations in central Mexico give an effect of massive solidity, further south in Yucatán the Maya developed a more slender, vertical thrust, and the pitch of the Mayan pyramid and its staircase are particularly steep.

The pyramid often rose over a tomb, and its inscriptions detailed events from ancestral history. The temple was a cosmic axis where the trunk of the World Tree rose out from Xibalba, the underworld. The hundreds of pyramids that rose toward the sky from their jungle clearings thus made the Mayan landscape into a forest of World Trees.

The Great Plaza and Temple II – the ceremonial heart of the Mayan city of Tikal, Guatemala (flourished c. AD300–800). The temple's roof-comb adds considerably to the impression of height.

The Mayan city of Palenque in southern Mexico, with the Temple of the Inscriptions at the centre, the Temple of the Sun on the left and the Palace on the right.

cated to Tlaloc, the rain and earth god, and represented the Mountain of Sustenance. The other temple, dedicated to Huitzilopochtli, the god of the sun and war, represented the mountain where the new-born god fought and destroyed his 400 half-brothers as they came to kill him and his mother. This may have been a metaphor for the daily battle between the sun and the moon as leader of 400 stars.

At sunrise and sunset a priest on the platform of the Templo Mayor would beat a loud drum to signify the start and end of the day's work throughout the city. The gap between the twin temples was aligned precisely to sunrise at the equinox when viewed from the circular temple of the serpent god Quetzalcóatl.

Some Mesoamerican pyramids – mainly in the Mayan area – were built over an underground burial chamber. Like those of the Egyptians, these pyramids were sometimes dedicated to the glorification of deceased rulers. The Mayan Temple of the Inscriptions (7th century AD) at Palenque, Mexico, contains a vaulted burial chamber in which

the great king Pacal was buried wearing a mosaic portrait mask made of jade, which symbolized life. Important burial chambers have been found elsewhere, including at Tikal in Guatemala.

Most Mesoamerican architecture has a strong frontal aspect and is designed to be viewed from outside. But at Chichén Itzá (see pp.16–17), Mayan architects developed the colonnade, allowing them to span a room with several vaults and to use wooden lintels to create large internal spaces. The result was a new conception of architecture as interior space, exemplified by the Temple of the Warriors – a pyramidal temple surrounded at ground level by colonnaded halls where large numbers of people could be received.

Mayan civilization was at its peak c.AD300–c.900, and the Maya carried Mesoamerican sacred architecture to its most elaborate and refined extent, as can be seen in the delicate sculpture of Copán and the painted stucco-work of Palenque. The Maya developed the corbel vault, in which stepped brickwork was built up to form an arch. In Mayan pyramids all effort was concentrated on the upward thrust of the architecture. The temples, which were entered only by priests, were often very small. The sense of height was increased by a distinctive "roof-comb".

Teotihuacan, Mexico

GULF OF MEXICO

● **Teotihuacan**
■ Mexico City

MEXICO

GUATEMALA

HONDURAS

PACIFIC OCEAN

This vast and mysterious site lies northeast of modern Mexico City. It was built (begun *c.*AD100), by an unknown people believed to be related to the Nahua. At one time the city housed up to 200,000 inhabitants. The economy was based on the control of trade routes, and the population was supported by irrigated agriculture. The city had no fortifications and no warlike motifs in its art, and the reasons for its collapse are as mysterious as its origins.

During the 7th and 8th centuries the monumental temples on top of the pyramids were systematically burned. Later, the abandoned city was regarded with awe by the Aztecs, who gave it its name ("birthplace of the gods"). They believed it to be where their gods Nanahuatzin and Tecuciztécatl had sacrificed themselves to become the Sun and Moon and bring into being the Fifth Creation (the present world).

The town is planned along a central avenue (the Avenue of the Dead), which runs for two miles (3.2 kilometres) north to south and contained some 100 religious buildings. Archeologists have so far identified 2,600 major structures laid out in a tight grid, each of which contained its own temple. The Avenue of the Dead is lined with numerous pyramids which were faced with roughly jointed stone blocks and finished with painted plaster rendering. The Aztecs named the most prominent of these the Pyramid of the Sun, and the next largest the Pyramid of the Moon.

ABOVE *The Pyramid of the Sun is 210 feet (63 metres) high and uses 2.5 million tons of material. A broad stairway leads to a platform, where once there would have been a temple. This pyramid is the culmination of an increasing concern with permanence in architecture – where the early Olmec mounds (1200–900BC) had been built of compressed soil or sun-dried brick,* the vast new pyramids were designed to last, with large stone retaining walls containing huge quantities of earth and rubble.

ABOVE *A carved head of the plumed serpent god Quetzalcóatl on a wall of the temple dedicated to him. Heads of Quetzalcóatl alternate with those of the rain god Tlaloc. The builders of Teotihuacan regarded Quetzalcóatl as a god of*

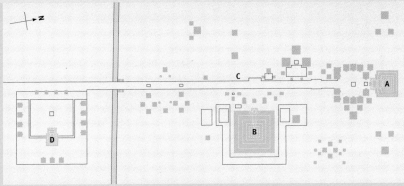

nature, but later the Aztecs identified him with the planet Venus and as a culture hero (a being that assists humans in their primeval struggles).
MAIN PICTURE, TOP *Lined with the remains of smaller structures, the Avenue of the Dead leads up to the Pyramid of the Moon, which, like many of the pyramids at Teotihuacan, echoes the shape of the mountain behind it.*

ABOVE *A plan of the main temples and pyramids of Teotihuacan. The Pyramid of the Moon (A) stands at one end of the long Avenue of the Dead (C), giving on to a plaza that would have been surrounded by smaller pyramids. The Pyramid of the Sun (B) is situated on the eastern side of the avenue, while toward the southern end is the temple of Quetzlcóatl (D).*

Greek temples

Against a rugged landscape of browns and greens, Greek temples stood out as white, sharp-edged geometrical shapes highlighted with red and blue. Buildings devoted to a single deity appeared around 800BC, in many shapes but already tending toward a rectangular hall (*megaron*). The great classical rectangular temples were mostly built between 600 and 300BC, following the invention of roof tiles and the replacement of earlier wooden material with stone. The god came increasingly to "dwell" in the temple in the form of a large statue, so that temple architecture evolved side by side with sculpture.

The god's statue stood in the hall or the sanctum and faced outward, usually east, so that it was lit by the rays of the rising sun. The congregation did not enter the sanctum but remained outside around the sacrificial altar, their activities watched by the statue of the god looking out through the entrance.

Rather than having arches, the Greek temple was trabeate (beamed) like the Egyptian temple, piling weight upon weight while avoiding outward thrust. The original *megaron* came to be surrounded on all four sides by a continuous row of columns (a peristyle). While the inner hall retained a solid wall breached only by one door, the columns of the surrounding peristyle provided a permeable and inviting boundary between inside and outside. Thus the temple was not an inward path like the Egyptian temple, nor a container of space like the mosque. Rather, the building encouraged movement around itself. With its triangles, rectangles and cylinders, it was designed to be seen from outside at all angles, and may be considered a work of sculpture. Architects were often supervised by sculptors, whose artistic visions they were realizing.

The temple of Segesta, Sicily, was never finished – the columns were not fluted and there was no inner chamber. From this we can see the way that Greek temples were built from the outside inward.

THE THREE ORDERS OF GREEK ARCHITECTURE

The styles of building in classical architecture distinguished by the capitals at the top of their columns are known as orders. The three principal orders of Greek architecture – Doric, Ionic and Corinthian – show an increasing ornamentation. Each was named after its region of origin, but they spread across the classical world and became elements in the overall repertoire of architecture, so that temples may contain elements of more than one order.

The Doric order is the oldest and simplest, originating between 1000 and 600BC. Doric columns are rooted directly in the earth and are topped by a capital shaped like a bowl. Some scholars think that the fluting imitates the bundle of papyrus reeds that supported the early Egyptian temple, with the capital as the block of wood that held the bundle together; others believe the fluting represents the strokes of the adze in stripping the trunk of a tree. The columns are often stout and the effect is heavy or massive. In the horizontal beam, square panels known as metopes alternate with triglyphs – panels with three vertical grooves, representing the ends of the cross-beams from the early period of wooden temples. Notable Doric temples are the Parthenon and the Theseum at Athens; the Temple of Poseidon at

Doric columns from the Temple of Poseidon at Paestum, southern Italy.

An Ionic capital from the ruins of the temple complex at Delphi, Greece.

A Corinthian capital from the Odeion of Agrippa in Athens, Greece.

Paestum in southern Italy; and the Temple of Athena in Syracuse, Sicily, now the Catholic cathedral (see pp.156–7).

Ionic temples appeared in the mid-5th century BC. They have more slender columns than the Doric, topped with a capital resembling tendrils, ram's horns or a swirl of water, and suggesting an upward energy. The columns are placed on a base and the fluting is narrow. The metopes and triglyphs have disappeared and are often replaced by a marble frieze, so that the Ionic temple is conceived as well as executed entirely in stone. Examples are the Erechtheum in Athens and many temples in coastal Turkey (the main Ionian region), such as the Temple of Artemis at Ephesus.

The Corinthian column, topped with a spray of carved acanthus leaves, is the most tree-like of the columns. According to legend, its inventor, Kallimakhos (late 5th century BC), saw these leaves twined round a basket of funeral offerings. Kallimakhos was a bronze-smith and the capital does indeed give the effect of metalwork. Unlike the Ionic capital, it can be viewed equally from all directions and it therefore allows more elaborate patterns of symmetry. The Corinthian column was used in the Temple of Olympian Zeus at Athens. It later became widespread and because of its exuberance was especially popular with the Romans.

The Parthenon, Athens

BULGARIA

ITALY

GREECE TURKEY

Parthenon ● Athens

MEDITERRANEAN SEA

The Parthenon was dedicated to Athena (the patron goddess of Athens) in her form as Athena Parthenos, the virgin. Commissioned by the Athenian leader Pericles, the temple was built *c.*447–432BC in the flush of victory over the Persians. It is widely revered as perhaps the most harmoniously perfect building in Europe.

The Parthenon crowns the Acropolis, the summit of the city and the site of the amphitheatre where classical drama was first performed. The geometrically regular buildings are set irregularly over the uneven rock – a sense of unity comes not from a single glance but from walking around the site.

The façade of the Parthenon is eight columns wide instead of the more usual six, so that the eye can never take in its whole width at once and must move across it repeatedly. Like the quick-witted goddess Athena whom it embodies, the nature of the Parthenon can never be grasped all at once.

Although the columns are Doric, the effect is light. Using sophisticated mathematics, the architects created deliberate irregularities in order to produce the overall effect of absolute evenness. These devices reinforce the feeling of an upward movement, and the entire temple seems to follow and complete the upward thrust of the hill itself.

The Parthenon survived largely intact until 1687, when it was severely damaged during bombardment by Venetian forces, leaving the ruins we see today.

ABOVE *In many Greek temples the columns swell slightly around the middle to correct the optical illusion that they are pinched inward, but in the Parthenon the columns also tilt slightly inward to avoid the illusion of falling outward. All the temple's horizontal lines are made to rise slightly toward the middle to counteract the impression of sagging.*

ABOVE *Horsemen ride into battle, a scene from the Parthenon's frieze. The architects of the Parthenon were subordinate to the master sculptor Phidias, and the building served as an exhibition hall for his sculptures. Carvings on the outer colonnade depicted, for example, battles among gods, Titans, Amazons and centaurs, and between the Greeks and the*

Trojans. The birth of Athena, who sprang fully formed from the forehead of Zeus, was also shown. On the outer walls of the inner chamber a continuous frieze portrayed the ordinary Greek citizens in a procession in honour of Athena. Many components of the frieze are now in the British Museum in London – the "Elgin Marbles" – and ownership is disputed by Greece.

ABOVE Despite its damaged state, the Parthenon dominates the hill of the Acropolis and is a looming presence above the city of Athens. To the left of the picture the remains of the Propylaea are visible: this was the gateway that led to the whole ceremonial precinct of the Acropolis. Beginning at sunrise, the festival processions in honour of Athena would wind their way up the rocky hill, through the Propylaea and into the sacred area, where as

well as the great Parthenon there were smaller temples, statues and free-standing altars.

ABOVE A 19th-century reconstruction of the Parthenon in cross section. In the naos (inner chamber) stood a vast statue of Athena, sculpted by Phidias in ivory and gold. Wearing a helmet and carrying a shield and spear, this represented the goddess in her form as warrior maiden.

Roman temples

The Temple of Bacchus at Baalbek, Lebanon (c. AD150–200), stands on a typical Roman high platform but has an unusual Greek peristyle of free-standing columns.

Early Roman temples were influenced by the local Etruscans (8th–3rd centuries BC), who had placed their temples on a very high base, so that they were approachable only up steps at the front. Even when the Romans came into direct contact with Greece, their temples retained this emphasis on a high and imposing frontage. While the Greek temple was designed to be viewed from all sides, many Roman temples seem almost two-dimensional, with steps and columns only at the front. Along the sides, columns may be attached to or even inset into the walls of an inner chamber (*cella*) taking up the entire width of the platform on which the

temple stands. The front porch was often built several rows of columns deep, giving a high, dominating aspect appropriate to the imperial period.

The Roman temple usually followed the basic Greek design of a rectangular building with an open-air altar in front, where burnt offerings were made and worshippers stood outside the front door. But the resemblance to the Greek temple is superficial. Roman engineering skills allowed architects to develop new techniques, so that they no longer thought only in rectangles and triangles. The invention of concrete and curved arches made it possible to construct an apse (arched semicircular recess) to hold

ROUND TEMPLES

The Temple of Vesta, one of the oldest temples in Rome, was a small circular building surrounded by a ring of Corinthian columns. Inside, this goddess of hearth and home had no statue, but her sacred flame was kept burning by six Vestal Virgins under a domed ceiling symbolizing the heavens. Near the temple stood an oak tree, on which the virgins hung their hair when it was cut off at their initiation. Thereafter they lived a life of strict chastity. Even in the grandest imperial time, the state cult of the domestic hearth took place in this tiny temple, which survives today only as a ruin.

The Temple of Hercules Victor (c.2nd century BC, restored 1st century AD) is the oldest surviving marble building in Rome.

Another round temple is the Temple of Hercules Victor, which was converted in the Middle Ages into a church, now dedicated to Santa Maria del Sole. This temple has often been confused with the more famous Temple of Vesta because of its unusual shape.

a statue of a god, and large interiors crowned with a dome. These features would later be carried over into the Christian basilica (see pp.124–5). Such interiors did not require supporting pillars. So although the Romans followed Greek styles and were especially fond of the flamboyant Corinthian pillars (see p.117), these were used more for decoration – free-standing or embedded in the walls – than out of structural necessity.

The Roman temple therefore turned the Greek temple inside-out, as temples came to be conceived and designed primarily as interior spaces rather than as sculptures facing outward. Some interiors became very large, although worship in any formal sense remained outside at the altar; the buildings were often used for political and administrative meetings. The interior itself became the Roman architect's main art-form, which reached its greatest achievement in the Pantheon (see pp.122–3).

While the Greek temple was designed in relation to the landscape, the Roman temple was often designed in terms of a centrally planned townscape. The forum at Rome, built under the emperor Augustus (ruled 27BC–AD14), used the temple façade to enclose a series of contrived vistas and views. This range of public buildings was conceived as a unified expression of state power. To the left and right were colonnades of shops, while the vista ahead was closed by the temple of Mars Ultor (Mars the Avenger) on a massive podium. The whole area was enclosed by a 100-foot (30-metre) high wall which disguised the built and natural surroundings beyond and created an interior space outdoors.

The Pantheon, Rome

The Pantheon in Rome was built by the emperor Hadrian around AD117–128. A conventional classical temple porch with Corinthian pillars leads into a circular hall, or rotunda, surmounted by an immense dome. This dome is a perfect half-sphere, its radius exactly equal to its height. In its centre there is a large circular hole, the oculus (eye), open to the sky and allowing sunlight, rain or snow to fall on to the marble floor beneath.

The name "Pantheon" indicates that the temple was dedicated to "all the gods". By Hadrian's time, such a dedication brought together a far wider range of deities than the old Greek-style Olympian gods of earlier temples. Roman religion was becoming less self-confident and more open to outside influences. As well as deified former emperors, it now included Middle Eastern gods or figures such as the Persian Mithras and the Judean Christ. The enormous scale of the Pantheon and its circular form emphasized the all-embracing nature of its theological and political symbolism. The building embodied a wholly new vision of a vast, multiracial empire, unified in the centralized Roman state and watched over by every conceivable divinity.

In 609, the Pantheon became the first temple in Rome to be converted to Christian use, and was dedicated to "all the martyrs". Still a church today, it is probably the world's oldest religious building in continuous use.

LEFT *Today the Pantheon is a Christian church – the niches that once contained Roman deities are now chapels and tombs, and the apse is the site of the main altar.*
ABOVE *The hemispherical dome is made of concrete, a Roman invention. Weighing 5,000 tons, it is supported on massive walls nearly 20 feet (six metres) thick. The height of the*

rotunda's drum is equal to its radius (approximately 70 feet; 22 metres). This in turn is equal to the radius of the dome, so that if the dome were continued as a sphere its bottom would just touch the floor. The interior is an all-embracing space with no focal point, giving the visitor a feeling of both immensity and great calm. A tremendous feat of design and engineering, the Pantheon epitomizes this high point of the Roman era.

ABOVE Interior of the Pantheon by Giovanni Paolo Panini, c.1750. This 18th-century painting demonstrates how the light fell through the oculus, as it still does today. Throughout the day, the sky god Jupiter was believed to be present in the form of this shaft of sunlight, which rotated slowly round the darkened walls. The floor was paved with a grid-pattern of different-coloured marble and granite brought

from all corners of the Roman Empire.

ABOVE The entrance to the Pantheon is a porch of granite Corinthian columns, with a plain pediment. The inscription cites Marcus Agrippa as the builder, but this refers to an earlier temple (27BC) on the same site. The effect of the dome inside is all the more breathtaking after entering through such a conventional porch.

Churches

The early Christians met in private houses, where their central rite was a shared meal – the Eucharist – in commemoration of Christ's last supper. This rite has remained central to the design of most later churches. After Christianity became the official religion of the Roman Empire in AD313, the basilica, a Roman public hall, was adopted by Christians. The royal connotations of this word (from *basileus*, king) were reflected in the use of the building, in which God was worshipped as emperor of heaven. The path of the nave led to the altar, but also beyond it to a throne, where the bishop sat – a practice that was abandoned only in the Middle Ages.

In western Europe the basic plan was the Latin cross, representing the cross of Christ. A long nave led from the west toward a shorter chancel in the east, where the altar was situated. The arms of the cross were formed by a transept. Large churches and cathedrals developed side chapels, ambulatories and areas for monks and pilgrims. An elaborate symbolism grew around the basic design. The northern arm of the transept, associated with darkness, cold and evil, was decorated with scenes from the Hebrew Scriptures (Old Testament); the southern arm, associated with light and warmth, depicted scenes from the New Testament. The path of the nave from west to east, culminating in the altar – the symbol of Christ's life – represented the passage from less to more sacred space, or from death to eternal life (see pp.134–5). This imagery was reinforced by the siting of the baptismal font, the symbolic start of a Christian life, at the west end by the entrance to the nave.

In the eastern Mediterranean, the design of the Byzantine church focused both architecture and worship on the dome (see pp.163, 166–7), which represented the vault of heaven. The dome was often centrally placed, typically in a Greek-cross plan in which the four arms are of equal length. The altar remained important, but came to be placed behind a screen, or iconostasis. Much mystical symbolism was

Church architecture is enormously varied worldwide. This 13th-century church in Lalibela, Ethiopia, is hewn out of the living rock.

The modern evangelical "Crystal Cathedral" in Los Angeles, made of glass and steel, is equipped with microphones and television cameras.

attached to its hidden position, inaccessible to lay worshippers (see pp.46–7).

A tension in Christianity between ritual and teaching is directly reflected in architecture. Many modern Protestant sects emphasize pulpits and lecterns rather than the altar, and abandon the sense of a path given by the nave in favour of a plan that is more like an auditorium (see pp.68–73). Some modern Catholic churches also follow this plan, but retain the focus on the altar.

Christian architecture reflects the opposition between grandiosity and humility, between the wealth of the established Church and the humble private rooms of the early Christians. The simplicity of the Quaker meeting-house (see p.42) with its lack of ritual is similarly found in Protestant mission huts in New Guinea and Africa today. Yet the royal imagery of the basilica may not be far away: in a simple Baptist meeting-house in India, while men and women sit separately on the floor, the pastor preaches from a wooden chair behind a table covered with a cloth and holy books. This is an unmistakable echo of the early basilica plan, in which Christ's deputies on earth sat on thrones behind the altar.

CHRIST PANTOCRATOR

The central dome of an Orthodox church is usually occupied by the figure of Christ Pantocrator, Ruler of All. Christ has his right hand raised in a gesture of blessing; the hand is turned toward the heart, indicating the inner knowledge that is given outward expression in an open book, containing quotations from the Gospels, in his left hand. The Pantocrator emphasizes Christ's cosmic role rather than his incarnation, and his halo therefore contains the three Greek letters that spell "The One Who Is". The Pantocrator also represents the Byzantine concept of Christ as the universal judge to whom all must render account, and his features are often stern. While painting in the West after the Renaissance uses perspective

The figure of Christ Pantocrator in the apse of the 13th-century church of Monreale, Sicily.

to open a window on to a world behind the foreground figures, Byzantine figures are presented without depth and look out on to the space in front of them. The worshipper who looks up into the dome is not a spectator but a servant confronted directly with the Lord.

St Peter's, Rome

The great basilica of St Peter's in Rome was commissioned in 1506 by Pope Julius II to replace the old St Peter's – outmoded and in disrepair – as a symbol of papal Rome. The new church was begun by the High Renaissance architect Donato Bramante, who designed a symmetrical Greek-cross plan with a large dome at the centre above the shrine of St Peter.

Bramante died in 1514, and construction barely progressed until 1546, when Michelangelo was appointed as architect. He modified the original plan with innovations such as giant two-story pillars, but kept the idea of a central dome. For its design he was inspired by Filippo Brunelleschi's earlier double-shelled dome (1420–36) for Florence Cathedral, with its elegant segments and ribs. Michelangelo died in 1564 and did not see the raising of his dome. The present, slightly pointed structure is a modification of the hemispherical shape that he had preferred, and was completed in 1590 by Giacomo della Porta.

In 1607, Carlo Maderno further revised the design of the basilica, using a traditional Latin-cross plan. He added a long nave, thereby increasing the size of the church to accommodate greater numbers of visitors. Maderno also erected the façade. The final architect to make his mark was Gianlorenzo Bernini, appointed in 1629. This great figure of the Baroque designed many architectural and sculptural details of the interior, as well as the piazza.

ABOVE *Statues of 140 saints are ranged along the entablature of Bernini's elegant colonnade.*
LEFT *Bernini took over as architect of St Peter's in 1629, by which time the classical restraint and balance of the Renaissance had given way to the decorative flourish of the Baroque. Bernini's masterstroke in St Peter's was the baldachin (ornamental canopy) at the meeting point of the*

four arms of the cross, above the tomb of St Peter. This fringed canopy of bronze hovers over the High Altar, deceptively weightless, at a height of almost 100 feet (30 metres), supported on four twisted columns twined with olive-tree foliage and crowned by angels.

RIGHT *This view of the interior shows the long, barrel-vaulted nave, and the baldachin under the great dome. The interior is richly embellished with sculptures and paintings of saints and allegorical figures.*

ABOVE *A view of the basilica and the piazza.*
Before his death, Michelangelo had designed a pillared porch and a temple front for the church. Adapting this plan, Maderno incorporated the temple front into his design for the façade, and provided five doors for the crowds to flow into the entrance-hall.

Bernini commenced his vast colonnade in

1656, commissioned by Pope Alexander VII to create a piazza worthy of the great church, and large enough to hold the pilgrimage crowds. Bernini took as his model the columns of the façade, echoing them with his covered porticos of smaller columns. Bernini described the two semi-circular arms of the colonnade as the motherly arms of the Church.

Boundaries, Thresholds and the Centre

In sacred architecture, humans arrange the materials provided by nature to create a special space within which they can encounter the divine. This space is marked off from ordinary space outside, echoing the way in which, in religious thought, the problem of evil and human suffering is widely seen as arising from a separation of humanity from divinity or wisdom. The goal of religion – to reunite oneself with the godhead – is mirrored in the structure of sacred buildings as they invite the worshipper to progress through them from a secular outer realm, through gateways and along paths, in a movement toward the centre – usually the most sacred part of the building. The approach may be guarded by barriers and monsters, in an architectural representation of the difficulty of the spiritual journey from separation to unity.

The sacred space of this pueblo church in New Mexico, USA, is separated from the outer, profane world by a gateway whose structure echoes that of the church and which is itself protected and sanctified by the image of the cross.

Inner and outer realms

Marking off an enclosed space sets up a distinction between what lies within and what lies without, and combines the human need for shelter with a powerful and widespread cosmological principle. Inside the home, the boundary may separate private from public space; at the edge of a jungle village, it may separate the human from the wild. The temple boundary marks off a holy, pure and powerful space from an outer space that is ordinary and unclean. This inner space is often so sacred that it can be reached only by degrees, as the visitor passes through successive barriers before reaching the innermost, and most sacred, point. Individuals must be purified before entering this space (see pp.62–3) and entry to the inner area is often permitted only to special categories of people.

A distinction between inner and outer realms is evident from the smallest to the largest scale. In one of the most basic forms of sacred architecture, common to many West African peoples, a diviner sits inside a circle of stones which no one else may enter. Similarly, village huts are often arranged in a circle with their entrances facing inward and the gaps between them closed by a fence that controls the inward and outward movement of people, animals and spirits alike. The Cheyenne of North America reflected their cosmology not only in the inner structure of the tipis but also in the arrangement of the camp in a circle with an opening to the east, the side

FORTIFIED SANCTUARIES

Fortified sanctuaries are found in many monastic traditions, such those of Tibetan Buddhism or Greek Orthodoxy. In Europe the fortified sanctuary combined monastic retreat from the world with the seat of a knightly order.

The most notable examples are sanctuaries dedicated to St Michael. The Christian associations of Michael as archangel and friend to pilgrims were mixed with earlier pagan legends of him as dragon-slayer and guide to the underworld. St Michael's sanctuaries are almost all found on rocky peaks or islets. The remoteness of these sanctuaries – such as Skellig Michael, off the west coast of

The fortified monastery of Mont St Michel (8th century), off the coast of Normandy, France, was a great pilgrimage centre. It is joined to the mainland by a narrow causeway.

Ireland, St Michael's Mount in Cornwall, England, and Sangra di San Michele in Piedmont, Italy – relates to the mystic revelation to be found in outer realms, where it is thought the divine may be spontaneously contacted.

The monastery of Gyantse, Tibet, built on a rocky outcrop. The outside world is kept at bay and the inner world protected by a fortified wall. The monastery both served and controlled the community.

from which new life entered, in the form of the sun. In large empires, it is often not simply the house or temple or even the city that is bounded, but the empire itself. The traditional Chinese city was built in a series of concentric rectangles, with the imperial residence occupying the innermost "box" – a city within a city. Far outside, the Great Wall marked the outer boundary, between the realms of civilization and of barbarian tribes.

Outer realms represent or contain a form of power that can be dangerous but that can sometimes be harnessed. A densely populated, urbanized inner realm can seem sordid and unclean, as opposed to the freshness of the country-side beyond. A sense of this underlies the modern Western appreciation of "nature" and is also seen in the wide-spread idea of the wilderness as a place of simplicity and spiritual purification, where nothing more elaborate than the hermit's hut or the makeshift initiation lodge is built. In this view, the wilder-ness is a source of power and strength which is brought back into the commu-nity – for example, in India, the hut of the forest hermit may be reproduced in the finial of a temple tower.

The most extreme Western idea of wilderness requires it to be an uninhab-ited area with no building whatever. But more commonly, points of special spiri-tual power are marked architecturally by shrines and pilgrimage sites. Here, within the wider outer realm, small areas of inner space are set up, and the shrines may reproduce in miniature the boundaries of the city.

Gateways, thresholds and openings

Gateways, thresholds and openings mark the transition between one kind of space and another. Crossing them can mark an individual's transition between different kinds of sacred or social state. For example, the Hindu god of thresholds is the elephant-headed Ganesh, and his statue or picture is often placed at doorways. But he is also the god of beginnings in a broader sense, and is worshipped at the start of any important

The doorway of a village house in Kansi province, China, decked with good-luck prayers.

undertaking, whether it be a wedding, a journey or a new business venture.

Openings such as doors and windows are a basic necessity, but they are also the most vulnerable parts of a building. The door represents the point at which entry is invited and can be controlled. Thresholds are often symbolic barriers at these openings, and they may be marked with prayers, spells and bless-ings aimed to ensure that such entry is benign and to protect the space within. The Chinese use spirit screens – short walls built just inside the gate – to repel demons. Or demon-like images can perform this function: in Buddhist temples, fearsome masks above the door are used to dispel evil.

In central Nepal, the *thelo* (threshold) separates the veranda from the interior. Special spikes are hammered into the threshold and into window-ledges, to guard magically against the entry of witches. Supposedly impure "castes" (for example, butchers, Muslims or Christians) are only allowed to cross the *thelo* as an exceptional favour, after which the house is purified. In some Arab areas, the threshold (*atabe*) takes the form of a long stone which forms an upward step: different levels mark a qualitative

ENTRANCE OF LIGHT

Light is perhaps the most fundamental metaphor in Islamic scripture. The Koran states: "God is the light of the heavens and the earth." Encoded in the "abstract" designs in Islamic architecture are figures representing sources of spiritual light –

The play of light and shadow through this carved window in the Amber Palace, Jaipur, India, forms an elaborate pattern of stars.

stars, lamps and rays – often entwined together with verses from the Koran, and located at doors, windows and prayer-alcoves.

Among the Kabylie Berbers of Algeria (see p.53) the door should remain open all day, so that sunlight can enter and bring prosperity. A closed door signifies sterility; to sit on the threshold, obstructing the sun, is to close off happiness and fertility. To say "May your door always be open" is a way of wishing someone well.

hierarchy between outer and inner space (see pp.130–31). The *atabe* is where shoes are left and where the visitor should wash. An identification may be made between the threshold and the household itself – in Mongolia, if anyone even inadvertently kicks the wooden threshold of the tent it is considered a symbolically aggressive act toward the family within.

Gateways make the most elaborate and explicit statements about controlling who may or may not enter a sacred space. From the Christian cathedral door on which the archbishop must knock, to the house of the Indian Sora people where the shaman's assistants break down the door to bring in an ancestral name for a baby, to the gates of the monasteries of Mount Athos which are barricaded from dusk until dawn, gateways control the identity and the timing of those who would enter.

Reflecting or proclaiming the perceived importance of what is inside the building, the door is often given exaggerated significance, marked by features such as arches, pillars or porticos. Many doors are fortified even when they have no military purpose – this can be seen in Europe where massive church doors are reinforced with iron. In China, the gateway was often the main element of the building and was protected by moats and towers. The head of a conquered enemy was buried beneath the gate, imbuing it with magical power; the headless victim was said to become its spirit guardian.

A door opens outward into the world as well as inward, and functions as an exit. The front step of the Arab threshold is also the place over which a corpse is laid for a while as the dead person leaves the house for the last time. In many parts of the world a back door releases garbage from the house and is explicitly likened to the house's anus.

A doorway in a monastery in Tibet. Auspicious and mythical animals are intertwined with lotus flowers and leaves to reinforce the propitiousness of the hall within.

Pathways

In architecture the pathway is the means by which people move in or between buildings. Its particular meaning – whether it is intended to lead to a focal point, encircle a holy site or meander along natural lines – is provided by the whole structure of which it is an element. The pathway is therefore not merely an incidental means of travelling from one place to another. It is an intrinsic part of the architecture, even when it is not itself "built".

The simplest constructions may contain implicit pathways, and to move along these is often to enact symbolic or mythical meanings. The circle of Stonehenge in England (see p.14), with its astronomical markers, formed several paths, as did the parallel passageways between the lines of stones at Carnac in France (see pp.84–5). The symbolic connotations of even a simple circular movement can be complex. The round dwelling (hogan, see p.62) of the North American Navajo is consecrated with a Blessingway chant, a ceremony that involves the participants moving round the "sunwise path", symbolically encircling the world. With the concave floor representing the earth (female) and the rounded roof the sky (male), the people circle the hearth clockwise, passing inside the four roof posts – a movement that also represents the passage of time, from sunrise to sunset.

The sacred pathway is also significant in the great temple complexes and cities of ancient civilizations. Many Mayan

The nave of Canterbury Cathedral, England. Lines of columns reaching up into the roof-vault create a pathway that leads the eyes and steps of the worshipper to the altar.

cities were linked by processional routes, or *sacbés*, used by priests and pilgrims. One such route on the Yucatán peninsula connected the cities of Izamal, Uci, Uxmal, Kabáh and Cobá. The Aztec capital, Tenochtitlán, built on an island in a lake, used canals as pathways to structure the city according to a divine ideogram. Four concentric pathways – representing the four main deities – demarcated the city's *barrios* (wards), with the ceremonial precinct at the centre. The city thus replicated universal space. In some cases the pathway demonstrated imperial divinity. In ancient Egypt during the New Kingdom (1570–1085BC) temples were linked by avenues of sphinxes, or Ways of God. Ramheaded sphinxes joined the temples of Amun and Khons at the complex of Karnak (see pp.90–91) – a symbol of generative power, the ram was sacred to Amun. The processional avenues of the New Kingdom, with their pylon gateways, colossal statues of the pharaohs and towering obelisks of red granite, celebrated the alliance of divine and earthly power.

Early Christians used the church building to embody the spiritual path of the believer. This is evident in the nave, the approach taken by the faithful to the altar, which represents a gradation from less sacred space at the west end to highly sanctified space at the east. Lines of pillars on either side evoke the sense of a path, and the depth given by the aisles behind them allows the pillars to stand in the round like tree-trunks in an avenue. The very shape of the nave seems to draw the devotee forward, and floor mosaics may also present patterns indicating forward movement. All these features draw together at the east and focus the eye on the destination, the altar.

SACRED PATHS TO CHINESE IMPERIAL TOMBS

From the early dynasties the tombs of Chinese emperors and generals were approached by avenues lined with images of guardians on either side. The earliest stone images are those of the Han Dynasty (2nd–1st centuries BC). The intrinsic qualities and shape of the stone were left evident, thus conveying the sense of permanence of stone itself. The carvings substituted the living guard of honour that lined the way for the emperor during his life and provided a permanent guard for him in death. The avenue often followed natural landscape contours to tap the sacred energies of nature (see pp. 28–9). Incorporating mythical creatures and auspicious beasts, it was also a symbolic link with the next world.

Camels and kneeling elephants line the avenue leading to the imperial tombs of the Ming Dynasty at Nanjing.

The Southern Dynasties (AD420–589) developed lively sculptures of pacing, grimacing and often winged beasts, and seem to have been primarily concerned with the supernatural power of such creatures. In the Tang and Song Dynasties (7th–13th centuries AD), the avenues incorporated figures from the living world, such as high bureaucrats and military officials. Sacred creatures also occur, including the lion and the kneeling elephant (symbols of power) and the ram (filial piety). The avenues of the Tang and Song create an image of the entire world to accompany the imperial ancestor in his afterlife.

Courtyards

The significance of the courtyard varies greatly from society to society. For example, a courtyard can close off a community from the outer world for the sake of spiritual purity; it can be a space of historically sanctified power; or it can be the source of domestic vitality.

The Christian cloister (see box), consisting of an arcaded walkway surrounding a garden, is often thought to have been foreshadowed in the Islamic East. But the rationale for the mosque courtyard (*sahn*) is quite different from that of the cloister. A dark corridor opens into the sunlight of the *sahn*, whose four walls symbolize the four columns that carry the celestial dome. The courtyard is thus linked architecturally to the sky or heavens. In the

centre of the *sahn* is an eight-sided fountain, echoing the octagonal shape of God's throne according to the Koran. The floor may be decorated with marble representations of fruit trees watered by rivers and streams. The whole courtyard represents paradise.

Moscow's Kremlin is a citadel courtyard; its walls are interspersed with towers and gates. It gained its sanctity by virtue of being the seat of the holy tsars, absolute rulers who were regarded almost as gods by many of their subjects. The Kremlin reflects a rejection of European modernization: its massive walls were erected in the 17th century, at a time when movements against autocracy resulted in the dismantling of city walls in the rest of Europe. Containing

The distinctive arcaded courtyard of the Great Mosque of Damascus, Syria (c.706–15). The walls of the mosque were originally covered with mosaics depicting a landscape probably representing paradise.

The Romanesque cloister of the 13th-century monastery of Santo Domingo de Silos, Spain. The columns are carved with biblical scenes, mystical beasts and abstract patterns, which the monks would ponder during their meditation.

THE CLOISTER

The Christian cloister was designed as a place of meditation for monks. In the 11th century at the Benedictine monastery of Cluny, France, the cloister became the chief architectural feature, due to expanding numbers and to the wish of each monk to have his own cell. The common dormitory had been abandoned almost everywhere by the late 14th century; individual cells were constructed around three sides of the cloister and joined in an integrated complex with the other buildings. Gradually the significance of the cloister changed, as the urge to give expression to communal meditation gave way to the need to create spaces for individual work. From their cells monks were often active in public life. In the 15th century, from his cell in the cloister at San Marco, the Dominican friar Savonarola roused the whole of Florence to revolt.

cathedrals, armouries, tombs, stables and gardens, the Kremlin constitutes a separate historical zone that is out of step with the rest of Moscow. Perhaps for this reason a statue of Lenin was never erected there, although such statues pepper the city. The Lenin statue symbolizes the timeless future of the Communist ideal – planners may have realized that it could not withstand the weight of historically legitimized sanctity represented by the Kremlin.

In West Africa the courtyard is the well-spring of life and fertility. Among the Ashante of Ghana it is the fundamental form of all traditional architecture, from palaces to shrines and houses. The courtyard house reflects the central role of the family in Ashante society. The yards are semi-private areas, used for the communal activities of a household. A sacred bush symbolizing life is planted in the centre. The temple shrine echoes this pattern: the single entrance leads to a sacred courtyard, surrounded by rooms with diverse functions, including the main shrine room and a drum room. Significantly, the Ashante tomb, the realm of death, is the architectural opposite of the courtyard, being open on all sides under a hanging roof.

The concept of the enclosed courtyard can also be applied to sites that would seem to be open by their very nature. The Zapotec city of Monte Albán in Mexico was built at the top of a steep hill, yet the artificially levelled plaza (mid-1st millennium AD) creates an immense enclosed area in defiance of its topographical setting. The many temples at the edge of the plaza, separating it from the precipitous slopes of the hill, allow virtually no view of the surrounding valleys but concentrate attention inward to the group of three temples at the plaza's centre.

Labyrinths and spirals

The earliest known labyrinth dates from the 19th century BC in Egypt, where it represented the path through the underworld. Labyrinths are also known in Buddhist thought, where they are intricate paths to enlightenment. But the archetypal labyrinth for European culture is that built, according to Greek myth, by Daedalus for Minos, King of Crete (see p.33). Here the labyrinth is a disorienting tangle of paths in which the unwary are lost, but which nevertheless contains a true path to the centre. In the myth, the Minotaur – part man, part bull – lurks in the depths of the labyrinth, devouring youths and maidens offered in sacrifice. The hero Theseus eventually finds his way to the centre and kills the monster. He is

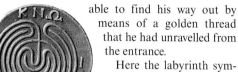

This coin (1st millennium BC) from Knossos depicts the labyrinth as the city's symbol.

able to find his way out by means of a golden thread that he had unravelled from the entrance.

Here the labyrinth symbolizes the idea of penetration, through an initiatory test of personal qualities, to the centre. Thus it came to be associated with spiritual progression and discovery of the self. Complicated and winding in form, the labyrinth nevertheless represents order to those who understand it but confusion to the uninitiated.

Unlike almost all other sacred architecture, the lowest level of the labyrinth has the greatest power. Archeological remains in Crete suggest that the mythic labyrinth may have been based on the Palace of Minos at Knossos, where the throne-room was like a sacred cavern.

The threshold stone at the entrance to the passage-grave at Newgrange, Ireland (see p.85). The paired spirals suggest opposed vortical energies, by which a state of balance is achieved.

The palace seems to have had an upper solar section, consecrated to life, and a lower lunar region, dedicated to death, reflecting the idea that death and the afterlife were religiously more important than life. This echoed the Egyptian labyrinth, where beneath an accessible cult area lay a subterranean region for secret rites and tombs, to which entry was forbidden to the uninitiated.

The sense of movement in finding one's way through a labyrinth is similar in many ways to the movement inherent in the spiral, as the writer Jill Purce has pointed out. The one true path, often seen as that of the pilgrim, culminates in an encounter with the divine. The idea of the labyrinth-spiral, coiling back on itself, has led to images of a two-way movement, with seekers after the truth going in one direction and angels or divine messages coming in the other. Mystics have pondered the idea that the end of the spiral is also a beginning, or that the spiral leads out of this mundane world altogether. Thus many cultures attribute spiritual significance to whirling, vortex-like dances, which generate extreme exaltation or an otherworldly trance state. The idea of the expansion of consciousness evoked by spiral ascent is seen throughout the world, perhaps most dramatically in the dynamically ascending spiral minaret of the 9th-century mosque at Samarra, Iraq (see frontispiece).

THE EUROPEAN MAZE

The idea of the labyrinth has long fascinated European minds. In early Christian thought the maze was a symbol of the path of ignorance, leading away from God. However, by the 13th century the labyrinth had come to have a positive symbolism, as the path of the pilgrim strewn with difficulties. By the 17th century the labyrinth was also reproduced in secular contexts, such as in the hedge-mazes of great villas, reflecting a popular concern with finding one's way to a goal.

The labyrinth-spiral is depicted in the pavement floors of many medieval cathedrals. In Chartres Cathedral, France, the 13th-century maze on the floor of the nave is located so that, if the wall containing the west rose-window were hinged at the ground and bent down, the window would cover the maze exactly. The maze has only one path to the centre. It represents a spiritual journey, the winding path of the soul through human life, while the rose-window depicts the Last Judgment, the fate of the soul after death. The maze, located at the beginning of the nave, also forms an initiatory barrier to the sacred realm at the altar.

The rose at the centre of the maze at Chartres is said by some to be above a powerful earth current, which exerts a force on those walking the maze.

The centre

The centre is not a literal geographical location but a cosmological concept that points to a focus of spiritual power, a place where space and time come together.

In vertical space, the centre is the point of opening from one level to another and is often represented in architecture as a pillar, *stupa*, mountain or ladder to heaven. Altars similarly constitute a centre, as the point at which a sacrifice can move between the plane of the earth and that of the gods. A centre can also lead downward. As well as reaching up to heaven, the Rock in Jerusalem holds down the chaotic waters in the abyss under the earth.

In horizontal space, the centre is the point from which the organized and habitable world takes its bearings. In ancient China, just as in the Aztec capital of Tenochtitlán and the Inca capital of Cuzco, it was not only the temple but the entire city that was called the centre of the world.

Relationships between sacred buildings and the concept of the centre are varied. The synagogue and the mosque each look to a single geographical centre as the site of a historical event. Conversely, Delphi was considered the "navel" of the Greek world (see pp. 142–3), yet Greek temples were not oriented toward Delphi.

Many traditions make it clear that the centre is not so much an absolute concept as a relational one, the point toward which a community's life, thought

The 7th-century AD shore temple at Mamallapuram in southern India is built to a centralized mandala *plan, and the tower at the centre represents Mount Meru.*

and activity are oriented. In these cultures there can be multiple centres, with each city, temple and house having its own pillars, altars and shrines. Nomadic Mongols even carry their centre around with them and re-establish it every time they set up their round tent with its central hearth under the smoke-hole leading directly to the sky (see pp.20–21).

The centre is not only a spatial concept, but also a point of origin in time. The Walbiri Aborigines of Australia erect an elaborately decorated post in a hole in the ground at a ceremony to increase the fertility of ants. As dancers move toward this pole across a series of concentric circles drawn on the ground they approach the point of contact with the Dream Time of the ancestors, which lies at the deepest part of the hole. In other cultures, rites of construction and consecration may project a sacred building into the centre of the universe by re-enacting the creation. Such rituals probably took place in ancient Sumeria in a divine drama at the consecration of the temple and its annual re-dedication.

This repetition in time and multiplicity in space show that although sacred buildings are a powerful spiritual focus, a degree of centrality can be created anywhere at any time. The power of the centre can be diffused and reproduced in pictures of shrines, gods and saints in homes, cafés and buses. Even one's own body can be a shrine and a centre – a *mandala* not only serves as a ground-plan for the Hindu temple but can also be internalized mentally, to make the body of the meditator into a microcosm of the universe. Ultimately the centre is not a building but a state of mind or a state of grace. As the labyrinth suggests (see pp.138–9), the journey to this understanding of the centre is difficult and dangerous. One of the main roles of sacred architecture is to guide the devotee toward this destination.

THE IMMOVABLE CENTRE

Judaism, like Islam (see pp.80–81, 96–7), is unusual in retaining one single centre for a large community of believers that is scattered throughout the world. It was the destruction of the Temple of Solomon (see pp.108–9) and the subsequent dispersal (diaspora) of the Jewish people that laid the historical foundations for this immovability, and no other religion has retained its focus on a centre through such historical vicissitudes. A rabbinical text, the Midrash Tanhuma, states that just as the navel is at the centre of the person, so the land of Israel is at the centre of the world, the city of Jerusalem at the centre of Israel, the Temple at the centre of Jerusalem, the Holy of Holies at the centre of the Temple, and the Ark at the centre of the Holy of Holies. In front of the Ark is the foundation stone of the world.

The site of Solomon's Temple, Jerusalem. According to one Jewish text, God created the world from this centre outward. The site is now occupied by the Dome of the Rock, a Muslim shrine (AD691).

Delphi, Greece

Delphi, on the spectacular slopes of Mount Parnassus, was the holiest place in ancient Greece. It was believed to be the navel (*omphalos*) of the world, the place where two eagles met when released by Zeus from opposite ends of the earth.

The sun god Apollo took over the site by conquering the Python, who was probably a form of the earth goddess. The Delphic oracle combined the powers of the male sun and the female earth. Apollo's temple was supposedly built over a cleft in the earth that gave out intoxicating fumes which threw the oracle priestess into her soothsaying trance. However, earthquakes have obliterated any trace of this cleft today.

According to legend, Apollo's temple was made first of beeswax and feathers, later of bronze, and finally of stone. During the 5th and 4th centuries BC the site grew into the greatest of all Greek oracles and even mighty foreign kings would come to ask their fortunes. Through pilgrims' fees and the offerings deposited by grateful clients, Delphi built up the richest collection of treasures in the Greek world.

The site's long inviolability was testimony to its role as a sacred centre among the endlessly warring Greek cities. But the treasures were plundered by the Roman emperor Nero in AD67, and after a long decline the oracle was finally shut down in AD393 by the Christian emperor Theodosius. The centre had moved elsewhere.

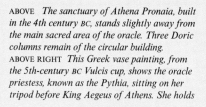

ABOVE *The sanctuary of Athena Pronaia, built in the 4th century BC, stands slightly away from the main sacred area of the oracle. Three Doric columns remain of the circular building.*

ABOVE RIGHT *This Greek vase painting, from the 5th-century BC Vulcis cup, shows the oracle priestess, known as the Pythia, sitting on her tripod before King Aegeus of Athens. She holds a bowl and a sprig of laurel or bay, and it was possibly through chewing these leaves that she attained the state of trance necessary for the god Apollo to speak through her.*

OPPOSITE LEFT *The omphalos stone – a rounded conical stone marking the navel of the world. The meaning of the carvings is not known. The stone is now in the museum at Delphi.*

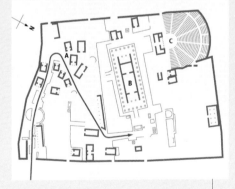

MAIN PICTURE, TOP *The Delphic oracle is situated amid precipitous mountains, from a cleft of which run the purifying waters of the Castalian spring. At the centre is the Temple of Apollo, now reduced by earthquakes to a few pillars; the oracle priestess sat in the temple's inner sanctum. Above the temple were a theatre – still well preserved – and a stadium.*

ABOVE *A plan of the* temenos *(sacred area): the paved "sacred way" (shown in red) zigzagged uphill to give a series of carefully planned views, each with its own emotional impact, past the offerings, statues and treasuries (A) of numerous individual cities, to the imposing Temple of Apollo (B). Behind this was the theatre (C).*

The Architecture of the Afterlife

Sacred architecture enlists society's greatest material and human resources to express the transcendent and the eternal through massive stonework and exquisite ornamentation. In traditional cultures where all other buildings are small and humble, such visions of immensity and permanence are overwhelming and present a vivid contrast to the frailty of humans.

Mortals can share a little in this permanence, and even aspire to divine status, through the construction of tombs. While sacred buildings are often modelled on the living human body, the tomb suggests that the person continues to exist after death, either in another world or in the minds of those left behind. But even tombs, like temples, will eventually crumble, leaving enigmatic ruins only partly understood by future generations.

The "City of the Dead" in Cairo is a series of cemeteries stretching over several miles. Because of Cairo's increasing population, many of the tombs and large mausolea are occupied by living squatters and are surrounded by shops and stalls, like a residential suburb. The tombs are still visited by the relatives of the dead, and the outings are often turned into picnics.

The needs of the dead

Tombs are the oldest known form of architecture, and some of the oldest known art was buried inside them. It seems that a main function of the early architect, as of the artist, was to provide for the needs of the deceased. This was based on the almost universal human belief that the dead continue to exist in some realm or dimension, and that communication and mutual support are possible between the dead and the living.

Much funeral architecture emphasizes the support that the dead will continue to need from this world. In many ancient civilizations the houses of the dead were more splendid than those of the living, which were built of mud and straw. Models or representations of useful everyday objects were buried and much of our knowledge of ancient ways of life comes from such burials. Egyptian tombs contain models of houses and food, while Han and Tang tombs in China are filled with terracotta models of soldiers, animals, servants, houses, granaries and wells.

In many traditions, real people and animals were sacrificed, and some tombs were large and many-chambered to accommodate these offerings. In 6th-century BC China, Confucius condemned this practice, and subsequently paper models replaced living creatures. A recently excavated burial platform of

Egyptian tombs were often richly decorated with scenes from daily life. The paintings in the hall of the tomb-chapel of Khety, governor of the Oryx province at Beni Hasan, Egypt (c.2050BC), include desert hunting scenes, and uniquely, on the rear walls, men wrestling.

the Moche in Peru revealed a chamber with a sumptuously dressed warrior-priest in a coffin, while in coffins alongside lay two presumed concubines, a dog and two guardians. Above in a separate chamber lay a further guardian. Several of the warrior-priest's attendants had had their feet amputated, as if to commit them to his service for eternity. At Pazyryk in Siberia, the 2,400-year-old tomb of a woman was excavated from the permafrost in 1993. The burial chamber, oriented from west to east, resembled an underground log cabin; the woman was buried in a coffin, with a meal beside her. The chamber was roofed over and several finely harnessed horses had been sacrificed and lowered down before the tomb was filled in. In this semi-nomadic

Over 6,000 life-size terracotta warriors, no two alike, were buried near the tomb of the emperor Shi Huangdi (c.259–210BC), Xian, China. The army, ready for battle, faces east, from where enemies had come.

society, the tomb was the only permanent building, in which time was frozen.

Funerary architecture aims to meet the needs of the dead, but also meets the emotional needs of the living. A photograph, death mask or lock of hair may be built into a tomb or memorial. Tombs may also be ornamented with statues of weeping figures. In Roman Egypt this led to a tradition of lifelike portraits painted on wood. In medieval Europe wax effigies of the deceased gave place to recumbent stone sculptures on tombs, giving the ephemeral human person a permanent architectural form.

MEGALITHS FOR THE DEAD

The standing stone is perhaps the simplest form of funerary architecture, but its meaning may be complex. The Sora of India use architecture to express continuity of lineage. The main house-post symbolizes the link from ancestors to descendants, and offerings are made at its foot. Immediately after cremation, a person's ashes are covered by a thatched roof on model house-posts. People are afraid to approach this temporary house, as the deceased is still a dangerous ghost.

A meal is prepared for the deceased on the megalith before it is planted upright.

The deceased becomes a full ancestor only after a series of rites, beginning with the "planting" of an upright memorial stone among the lineage's group of standing stones. The deceased is fed at this stone with wine and the blood of sacrificed buffalo, and in return gives his or her name to a new baby. The stone summarizes the full range of the dead person's needs; the buffalo are not only food but are also used for ploughing in the underworld. The buffalo and the stone are sometimes anointed and addressed as though they were the dead person.

Tombs

The labour required to construct the three massive pyramids at Giza almost defies imagination, yet they were all built in less than a century (c.2690–2600BC), possibly as a political gesture.

Sacred buildings are seen in many traditions as the means of salvation or rebirth for the dead. Thus the tomb and the temple are often combined – monarchs and great poets are buried at London's Westminster Abbey, and Muslim tombs in India often have a *mihrab* (prayer niche) built into the western wall of the main hall as in a mosque.

The shape of tombs may express a belief in rebirth, as in the megalithic passage-grave (see p.85). The sarcophagus, as container of the body, can resemble both a womb and the entire cosmos. To emphasize such cosmic significance, Egyptian coffins often had an image of the sky goddess Nut painted on the inside of the lid. In Mesoamerican architecture, the sarcophagus of the 7th-century Mayan king Pacal was shaped like a uterus. The pyramidal Temple of the Inscriptions (see p.113) beneath which Pacal's tomb is situated reflects the Mayan conception of the cosmos, with nine outer terraces symbolizing the nine layers of the underworld, and 13 internal strata corresponding to the 13 levels of the heavens.

A belief in the continuing power, as well as the needs, of the dead person underlies much tomb architecture. Christian shrines often contain sculptured effigies of saints, and the embalmed body of a saint may even be enshrined inside an altar.

Some of the most spectacular tombs ever constructed are the pyramids of Egypt. Early tombs were pits in the earth and any superstructure above ground has disappeared. From the 1st Dynasty (*c*.3000–2800BC), this underground chamber began to be covered with a long, low mud-brick platform, now called a mastaba. Many of these are found at Saqqara, the necropolis of Memphis, which is also the site of the best-preserved example of the next stage of development, the step pyramid of Djoser (see p.22). The greatest of the later "true" pyramids are those built at Giza in the 4th Dynasty (c.2625–2585 BC) by the pharaohs Khufu, Khafre and Menkhaure (Cheops, Chephren and Mycerinus). Khufu's Great Pyramid, the focal point of a huge funerary complex, rose to a height of 481 feet (147 metres). Pyramids were sealed after burial, and worship of the dead pharaoh took place in a temple at the foot of the pyramid. The mastaba tombs of other royalty and courtiers were nearby, sometimes laid out in rows like streets.

Although the pyramids remain mysterious, it is clear that they bring together ideas of permanence and rebirth through the use of astronomy, in the service of a divine kingship. As with Egyptian painting, the conception of the pyramid is two-dimensional, and the building was designed to be seen from the side. Above its square base, the pyramid gives a feeling of both ascent and descent, contraction and expansion. It thrusts upward like a staircase to the sky, while the rays of the sun god spread out from the apex to the earth.

The mummified body of the king was preserved in an inner chamber. Near the

THE CATACOMBS

The greatest network of catacombs in the Mediterranean area is that of the Christian cemeteries dug out of the soft volcanic tufa under Rome. These form a maze of underground galleries on many levels, lined with rows of rectangular niches, in which bodies were laid wrapped in shrouds and coated with lime. Occasional larger recesses served as family vaults.

The earliest catacombs date back to the 2nd century AD. Although the persecution of Christians continued until the early 4th century, the pagan Romans seem to have avoided desecrating them even when their location was known. Modern exploration of the catacombs dates from the 16th century, and new ones are still sometimes discovered during excavations for the foundations of buildings and underground railways.

The need to preserve the body was motivated by the Christian expectation of bodily resurrection at the Last Judgment. Catacombs were also used for secret prayer-meetings, memorial services and the celebration of the Eucharist. Believers tended the bodies of their own dead, while the community paid particular care to the bodies of saints and martyrs. Painted decorations often depict the raising of the dead Lazarus from his cave, and one of the many graffiti states: "There is light in this darkness, there is music in these tombs."

A gallery on the first floor of the Catacomb of Priscilla, showing the rows of niches like bunk-beds where wrapped bodies were laid.

pyramids were pits designed to hold boats. The king was thought to travel to the underworld in a boat and, like the sun god, to be reborn. Evidence also suggests a religion oriented to the cycles of disappearance and reappearance of the stars. Narrow shafts leading at precise angles from the burial chamber to the outside of Khufu's Great Pyramid are oriented to the stars of Orion's belt, which were linked to the god Osiris, who was murdered and was reborn.

Free-standing tombs are sometimes built as miniature replicas of temples or churches. In the West, burial has become increasingly secularized since the Industrial Revolution. The problem of where to bury the new mass urban population led to one proposal, in 1829, to build a pyramid for the people in London which would be four times higher than St Paul's Cathedral and hold ten million coffins. This pyramid was not built, but the need for more space, together with new ideas of hygiene, led by the late 19th century to landscaped suburban cemeteries with only a small chapel attached. Today, these cemeteries are being widely replaced by the even more compact and hygienic crematoria – a minimalist approach to funeral architecture not seen in many cultures since the early days of hunter-gatherers.

A Muslim tombstone in Istanbul, Turkey, in the shape of a turban. Such carvings denote the status of the deceased.

MUSLIM TOMBS IN INDIA

Developing from the 13th century onward, the Muslim tomb was a new type of structure in India. Hindus had generally cast ashes into sacred rivers, and early Islam had prohibited the building of tombs. Muslim royal tombs were housed in spectacular buildings, surrounded by exquisite formal gardens. The southern suburbs of Delhi are sprinkled with large and small domes of various dynasties in differing styles. Around the ruins of Golconda near Hyderabad in southern India rise numerous royal tombs. There, the bases of the domes were constricted, giving a bubble shape, with a second, lower ceiling inside the main chamber. Today, the rock-strewn landscape is virtually deserted.

In its most elaborate form the main chamber (*huzrah* or *estanah*) resembled the prayer-hall of a mosque. It was raised on a huge platform and contained a stone cenotaph in the middle of the floor, while the body was placed in a crypt (*maqbarah* or *takhana*) below. The Taj Mahal (1632–54), on the river Jumna at Agra, was built by the emperor Shah Jahan for his favourite wife Arjuand Banu Begum (Mumtaz Mahal), and is widely regarded as the most perfect of all Muslim tombs. The main hall is square in plan and the building's width is equal to its height. The height of the façade is equal to that of the dome, which swells as a bubble made from part of a sphere resting on a circular drum and capped with a finial. The effect of absolute tranquillity induced by the perfect proportions is emphasized by the symmetry of surrounding buildings and gardens. Islamic architecture in India generally replaced the glazed tile finish of Iranian models with materials such as marble and red sandstone. The Taj Mahal is faced in white marble which takes on different tones of light according to the time of day, sometimes seeming as translucent as pearl. Shah Jahan planned a similar tomb in black marble for himself across the river, but this was never built and he was buried alongside his beloved consort.

The perfect symmetry of the Taj Mahal is reinforced by its reflection in a still pool.

Toraja rock-cut tombs, Indonesia

CELEBES SEA

BORNEO

SULAWESI

Toraja area

JAVA SEA

BANDA SEA

Among the Toraja of Sulawesi in Indonesia, an elaborate series of rites must be held before a deceased person can become a benign ancestor, protecting the rice crop. Although today the Toraja are predominantly Christian, traditional funerals are still the usual custom.

The corpse is carefully clothed, and sacrificed buffalo are offered to the deceased person. A menhir (standing stone) is erected for each person who dies, and is placed with the other such menhirs that have accumulated over the generations, forming rows or circles reminiscent of the ancient megaliths of northwestern Europe. The body is kept near the menhirs in a "corpse-tower" constructed out of wood and bamboo in the form of a Toraja house, with a saddle-shaped roof and upswept gable ends. The corpse-tower is built on several levels and the corpse is laid on the first floor. During the funeral rites the death-priest and his female attendants sit on the second floor. Ritual dances are performed in front of the tower.

The corpse is then interred in a family tomb, cut into a cliff-face. These chambers have square entrances sealed with wooden doors and are reached by means of bamboo ladders. The cutting of the rock is carried out by specialists. The family places an effigy of the deceased, called a *tau-tau*, outside the tomb – this joins the other *tau-taus* leaning on a balustrade and surveying the rice fields that stretch into the distance.

LEFT *The corpse is transported to its burial place in a bier, which, like the corpse-tower, bears a striking and deliberate resemblance to the style of Toraja houses. The biers are extremely large and heavy, usually requiring some 40 men to carry them.*

ABOVE *A funeral procession winds its way in front of traditional Toraja houses. The women*

are bearing gifts for the family of the deceased.
The exchange of gifts at funerals creates endless
cycles of social obligation, thus reinforcing the
continuation of traditional customs even by
Christians. Funeral parties often last for many
days and are lavish affairs, frequently involving
hundreds of people. During the funeral rituals,
a great number of animals are sacrificed, so
that their souls may accompany the deceased
into the afterlife.

ABOVE *The corpse is eventually interred in a*
chamber cut in a sheer cliff-face. The chambers
are sealed with wooden doors, some of which are
ornately carved or painted; after the corpse has
been interred the doors are often hung with the
deceased person's belongings. These burial
chambers are family graves, and cutting them
out of the rock – considered unhealthy work –
can take several weeks or months. The bamboo
ladder by which the graves are reached is later
removed, leaving them inaccessible once more.
The tomb is referred to as the "house from which
no smoke climbs". In Toraja cosmology,
ascending smoke is associated with the east and

with auspicious rituals of fertility, while
descending smoke is associated with the west
and with the recently dead.

ABOVE *An almost life-size effigy or tau-tau is*
placed near the burial chamber, kept in place by
a balustrade of wood or rock. The tau-tau
represents the deceased and is fed with offerings
of food and betel-nut.

Public memorials

In an impermanent world, no kind of structure expresses the concern with permanence more single-mindedly than the public memorial. Architecturally, it is usually simple, and designed to be conspicuous from afar, like a cairn. Such memorials are generally conceived not as interior space, but as sculptures to be experienced from outside.

Many memorials amount to a specialized form of the tomb, embodying collective ideals and values. While ancient memorials often affirm the regenerative power of the deaths of kings, heroes and gods (see pp.148–51), the 20th-century war memorial opens up a very different vision of the death of the ordinary person. In the centre of almost every village in Western Europe, earlier religious monuments have been replaced since World War I by public memorials that list the names, ranks and dates of all the local people who

The sculpted tomb is an element of the vast Canadian World War I memorial at Vimy, France.

COSMIC GEOMETRY AND ARCHITECTURE

The quest for geometric perfection can sometimes be so intense that it stretches architecture to its limits. The Greek philosopher Pythagoras (c.560–480BC) developed the theory of the harmony of the spheres and attributed mystical significance to numbers. His tomb, discovered in the 1st century BC by Cicero, consisted of a perfect sphere balanced on the tip of a cone.

During the French revolutionary period, numerous fantastic proposals appeared for a memorial to Isaac Newton, who had died in 1727. These – all unbuilt – drew on the contemporary fascination with the form of the sphere, which was seen to represent equality as well as eternity. A design by Étienne-Louis Boullée consisted of an immense sphere containing nothing but a sarcophagus, under a vault pierced with tiny star-shaped holes for light.

Boullée's design for Newton's cenotaph (1784) was on a huge scale – the radial band is planted with trees.

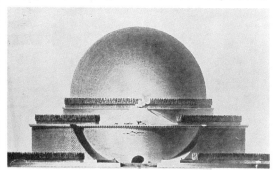

died. The effect is virtually that of a new ancestor cult. In France the war memorial took over almost completely from church altars dedicated to souls in purgatory, and in de-Christianized communities it is now the only architecture with a regular cult. Where village monuments had used the fountain, the crucifix and the Virgin Mary, the war memorial introduced pagan forms such as the menhir, the obelisk and the pyramid. These forms echo the memorial stone of the ancient Greek soldier, but also incorporate powerful Christian imagery, with the role of the martyr taken over by the suffering soldier.

Unlike many sacred buildings, 20th-century war memorials are not comfortable places to contemplate the cycle of life and death or the perfection of the divine. From the simple village memorial to the elaborate monumental complex, they emphasize the desolation and waste of war. In other cases, monuments glorify the victors' political system. On hills outside the cities of the former Soviet Union stand numerous colossal winged female figures holding swords and wreaths, partly to lament the deaths of millions but also to assert the superiority of communism over fascism. Similar monuments in Western Europe and North America glorify democracy.

Some war memorials are built out of the very materials of destruction, using shell-cases to make ornamental fences or converting a submarine, as at Kiel in Germany. Outside the headquarters of the United Nations in New York is a monument to the end of the Cold War made out of Soviet and US missiles – a "memorial" to a much-feared war that never took place.

DISPOSABLE MEMORIALS

A monument does not have to be permanent. It may also express transition, and hence continuity, through the very process of being destroyed. The Vikings placed the body of an important person in a ship, set it alight and pushed it out to sea. Members of the Thai royal family are cremated on a huge wooden pyre built in tiers of concentric terraces representing Mount Meru. The ashes become important relics to underpin the spiritual and political legitimacy of the next king. The unburned lower layers of the pyre, having fulfilled their purpose, are abandoned.

The funeral monument to the mother of the king of Thailand, who died in 1995. The coffin is visible in the centre. Once the Thai people had paid their respects the structure was set alight.

Defying time: the afterlife of monuments

Ancient monuments are often misunderstood, neglected or desecrated by subsequent generations. Yet a sense of continuing sacredness and power may be felt, and buildings are adapted to fulfil the needs of a new theology or belief. Sometimes this is done with a minimum of architectural adaptation, as with the Pantheon in Rome (see pp.122–3). At other times there is considerable change, as when a church was built at the centre of power in the pagan stone circle at Avebury (see pp.86–7), or when the cathedral and central square in Mexico City were established on the site of the 25 temples of the Aztec sacred enclosure in Tenochtitlán. Sacredness can also be

perceived as cumulative. The place where the Dome of the Rock in Jerusalem now stands as a Muslim shrine has been the site of Adam's tomb, Abraham's sacrifice of Isaac, Solomon's Temple, and Muhammad's ascent to Allah.

The investment of labour and materials in a sacred building also encourages re-use. The Temple of Athena at Syracuse in Sicily, built in the 5th century BC, was turned into a Christian cathedral in the 7th century AD. The conversion from Greek temple as exterior sculpture to cathedral as interior space was achieved by turning the temple outside-in (see opposite).

Buildings that lose their believers do

CÓRDOBA CATHEDRAL

The cathedral at Córdoba in southern Spain was originally a pagan temple to the Roman god Janus, and later dedicated

by the Christianized Visigoths to St Vincent. The Moorish ruler Abd ar-Rahman replaced the church with a mosque in 785, locating the *mihrab* over the end of the

former nave. The mosque eventually became the largest in the world after the Kaaba at Mecca (see pp.80–81), with a unique forest of marble pillars. The Christian king Ferdinand III reconsecrated the building in 1236 to the Assumption of the Virgin. In 1523, the local clergy demolished the central part of the mosque's prayer-hall to make way for the cathedral that now rears up above the low roof. Later, the Spanish emperor Charles V bitterly regretted this conversion, saying, "what you are doing here can be found everywhere, and what you possessed previously existed nowhere". Today, Roman, Visigothic, Moorish and Baroque styles combine in one of the world's most breathtaking and multi-layered sacred buildings.

Córdoba's hall of columns, part of the original mosque.

Syracuse Cathedral, Sicily, formerly the Temple of Athena. The solid wall of the original inner chamber was cut through to produce an arcade which formed a nave (left), while the spaces between the columns of the outer peristyle were filled in to create a solid external wall (right).

not always find new sacred uses. Abandoned churches become homes, village halls and cinemas – even a fudge factory. While churches are deconsecrated, many sacred buildings are merely overtaken by time. The Egyptian and Mayan temples survived when their civilizations vanished, and now bear witness to a religion that is no longer fully understood.

To express the divine in the solid materials of architecture is an astonishing feat of human creativity. The continuity of symbolism and design in each architectural tradition is evidence of the attempt to hold on to spiritual insights. Yet the ruins of numerous civilizations testify to the eventual demise of all specific religions and values, an end to all built representations of eternity. A building gives visible and tangible form to an idea of the divine, holds it awhile, and loses it again. Other traditions may recapture the idea, but in a different form. Since Cicero found the tomb of Pythagoras (see p.154) it has been lost again; but the cosmic geometry it expressed lives on as the foundation of mathematics and harmony, emerging repeatedly in the various traditions of sacred architecture.

OVERLEAF *The buildings of the 12th-century temple of Angkor Wat, Cambodia, crumbling with time, are gradually overgrown by the great roots of the strangler figs.*

Documentary Reference

Techniques of building

Up until the past few centuries, almost all large buildings
had either a sacred or a royal function or purpose. To
mobilize the wealth and labour necessary for construction
required the authority of the state and of its divine king. In
ancient civilizations the categories of secular and sacred,
temple and palace were not as distinct as they are in the
West today. The techniques of sacred architecture were thus
those of any large-scale architecture, and the main technical
challenges were in the struggle to achieve size and height in
the face of the force of gravity.

Sacred architecture expresses ideas of the divine in
material form, so that every aspect of style and structure
tends to be intensely imbued with theological meaning. But
a structure is constrained by the limitations of technology
and materials – as can be seen in West African "anthill"
mosques, which are built of mud (see p.97). This is perhaps
why many styles give a feeling, not simply of upward
achievement, but of an effort behind this achievement which
strains to the very limits of human capability. Not
infrequently, architects overreached themselves and their
towers collapsed.

The stylistic evolution of buildings is inseparable from
their technical development. A dome, for example, will be
supported in a way that reflects the integration of local styles
and technology. Where there are no modern engineering
models or computer simulations of force and stress, each
previous building serves as a model for the next and acts as a
starting point from which to make minor adjustments and
adaptations to local conditions and materials. However, style
may lag behind technology: what was a structural necessity
in an obsolete technology often persists under a new
technology as an element of ornamentation. The anthill
shape of mud mosques is preserved in mosques made of
cement, just as Greek architects continued to reproduce the
ends of wooden beams in the triglyph of the stone temple.

OPPOSITE *The ambulatory of
the cathedral of St-Etienne at
Bourges, France (12th–13th
century), showing typical
Gothic stained-glass windows
and diagonal ribs (see p.168).*

CONCEIVING AND EXPERIENCING
A SACRED BUILDING

LEFT *The plan of the Buddhist temple at Borobudur in Java. When seen in elevation (see pp.24–5), the temple resembles the cosmic mountain. The plan, however, reveals the* mandala *form that underlies the structure. At the same time as moving upward to the summit, the visitor moves from the outer edge of the cosmos to the centre.*

The ground-plan represents a building on a horizontal plane, showing its point of contact with the ground on which it stands. It is from here that the building's mass must thrust itself up against the forces of gravity. In sacred architecture, the plan is the god's-eye view, and indeed gods are often called architects, as if the universe itself were a huge building. Some plans, such as the *mandala* (see pp.12–13), are conceived as reproducing the shape of the universe.

But the plan is only two-dimensional. The third dimension – height – is indicated by elevation and section. The elevation shows an exterior façade from one particular point of view, while the section slices vertically through the interior of a building to show the sequence and proportions of the rooms inside. Many alternative elevations are possible for any given plan, as is shown by the greatly varied reconstructions proposed by archeologists in cases where nothing has survived of a building except the foundations.

Plan, elevation and section are related to the sense of sight, but they are primarily concepts. The full experience of a sacred building calls on all the senses as a person walks around, moving through a series of rooms, corridors, court-yards and halls or a succession of light and dark spaces, up into a dome or down into a crypt. Feelings of liberation or confinement can be enhanced by smells, the touch of stone, or the sounds of echoing footsteps and distant music.

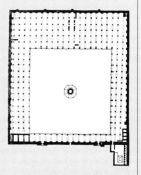

ABOVE *Plan of the Mosque of 'Amr, Old Cairo, Egypt. While the* mandala *(above left) reproduces the totality of the cosmos and holds the centre within itself, here the centre of the world lies far outside the mosque. The dot in the centre is simply a fountain, and the plan's significance can only be interpreted if the theology behind it is understood.*

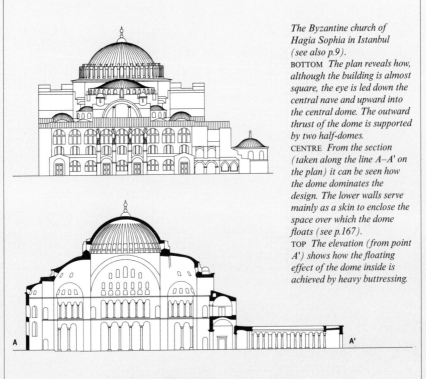

The Byzantine church of
Hagia Sophia in Istanbul
(see also p.9).
BOTTOM The plan reveals how,
although the building is almost
square, the eye is led down the
central nave and upward into
the central dome. The outward
thrust of the dome is supported
by two half-domes.
CENTRE From the section
(taken along the line A–A' on
the plan) it can be seen how
the dome dominates the
design. The lower walls serve
mainly as a skin to enclose the
space over which the dome
floats (see p.167).
TOP The elevation (from point
A') shows how the floating
effect of the dome inside is
achieved by heavy buttressing.

A   A'

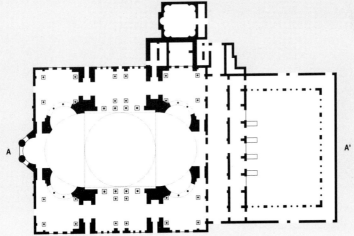

A   A'

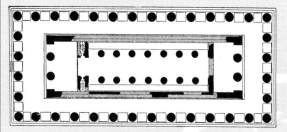

Plan of the Greek Temple of Poseidon at Paestum, southern Italy (c.475–450BC). The elongated central hall (naos) contained the god's statue; the small chambers to left and right are the entrance hall and the treasury respectively. The entire central building (sekos) is surrounded by a peristyle of Doric columns, like a perforated screen that draws the eye inward from afar.

So although the building is stationary it must be experienced in time, through a person's movement. Such movement is through two kinds of space, which the architectural historian J.G. Davies calls "paths" and "places". A path, as exemplified by a nave, an aisle or a labyrinth, has edges, direction and destination, and suggests a journey or a quest. A place, by contrast, is a concentration or focal point, a non-directional point of rest, such as the interior of the prayer-hall of a mosque. The alternation of path and place is fundamental to the rhythm of a building – for example, movement along a path may lead the worshipper to a still centre for contemplation.

Davies also explains how sacred buildings are "mass-positive", "surface-positive" and "space-positive", according to how far they stress these three aspects. Architectural traditions vary in their emphasis on each of these and buildings may combine mass, surface and space in numerous ways. A building that emphasizes mass has a sculptural quality, like the Greek temple, where it is the solid elements that are important rather than the voids in between. Such a mass-positive building invites experience through touch and its essence is revealed on a plan by the solid lines and dots which represent the walls and columns.

A surface-positive building accentuates the planes that bound the building's internal space, as in the solid façades of the Egyptian temple. The result may feel somewhat two-dimensional, but such surfaces often serve as a ground for highly elaborate decoration with tiles or sculptured reliefs.

A space-positive building captures space or volume in a special way and makes effective use of all three dimensions. Perhaps the supreme example is the Byzantine dome (see pp.166–7), which can appear to hover almost weightlessly over the hall beneath. The essence of such a building can be detected on the plan, not so much in the lines and dots that signify the walls and columns, but in the gaps between them.

The Latin-cross plan of Pisa Cathedral, Italy. A transept cuts across the nave at right angles to symbolize the cross of Christ. Because they obviously do not lead anywhere further, the arms enhance the sense of a single onward journey toward the sanctuary at the eastern end (top).

HEIGHT AND LIGHT: FROM CAVE ROOF
TO VAULT OF HEAVEN

A repeated theme in monumental sacred architecture is the struggle to create large internal spaces and give them height – to produce something similar to the archetypal cave, but reaching into the sky. This has traditionally been achieved according to two main technical principles, which may be called static and dynamic.

The static is based on the lintel, architrave and corbel (see glossary). Involving the use of uprights and cross-beams, this is the simplest technique, and the earliest in every tradition, especially where wood for beams was plentiful. It is found in the Egypt of the pharaohs, in classical Greece, in India before the Muslims, in the wooden temples of Japan and China, and in most Mesoamerican architecture. In the simplest trabeate, or post-and-beam system, horizontal

Semicircular Romanesque arches at the 12th-century Abbey of Vézelay, France. The Romanesque style replaced earlier wooden ceilings with a stone vault. The effect was to make the building's structure more complex, as arches across the nave broke up any rapid movement of the eye toward the sanctuary, while arches along the side enabled the construction of bays leading out into the aisles. Four arches at right angles are linked by a groin vault (the intersection of two vaults). The height of the Romanesque arch above its supporting pillars was limited to the radius of the arch, unlike the later Gothic arch which was no longer constrained by the geometry of the circle (see p.168).

beams with their downward force are held in place by the upward thrust of posts or columns. All architecture with columns is based on this principle, or imitates it. The width of an interior space is limited because a beam cannot stretch far without needing the support of a further pillar.

The dynamic technique uses a principle of thrust and counter-thrust based on the arch, vault or dome. It was sometimes used where timber was not available, as in the igloo of the Arctic regions or the mud-brick buildings of ancient Mesopotamia. But the large-scale arch and dome in stone originated in the Hellenistic (late Greek) and Roman periods, from where they later spread into most Christian and Islamic regions and styles. The arch can span a wider distance than a beam can because its rise generates horizontal as well as vertical forces, so that some of its weight is transferred to its central point and the two curves of the arch support each other.

The interior of the dome of the Sultan Ahmet Mosque (Blue Mosque) in Istanbul (see also p.49) showing the supporting pendentives. The architect developed the Byzantine dome and enhanced the effect of ethereal brightness by placing bands of windows around the main dome and the four subsidiary half-domes beneath.

Where the arch is continued for some depth, forming a ceiling, this is called a vault. Where it is rotated on itself through 360 degrees, the result is the dome, which resembles the way that humans perceive the sky. As well as representing a distinctive technical achievement in the Mediterranean and Middle Eastern regions, the dome is appropriate for the sacred architecture of those areas because both Christianity and Islam conceive of the sky as the residence of God.

In building a dome the technical problems of how to support it must be overcome, as must the theological challenge of how to emphasize its significance as a model of the heavens. For all its engineering accomplishment, the dome of the Pantheon in Rome (see pp.122–3) was simply a lid on a cylindrical building. The later dome of Byzantine churches was conceived in a more subtle way as a baldachin – a hemispherical canopy like an umbrella. This was supported on four columns, which linked the circular dome to the square base of the building beneath. The dome dominates and defines the shape of the interior space overall, so that the walls in between the four supports become insubstantial, almost like curtains – or even optional. The emphasis is not on mass or surface, but on space itself, which seems to radiate down from a hovering dome, just as in Christian theology heaven descends to earth.

The baldachin serves to show how ornamentation in a sacred building is not just decoration for its own sake, but grows out of the very form of the building. The Byzantine dome is often supported on four pendentives. The pendentive is a curved triangle at the point where the dome meets its supporting pillars. It appears to be caught up in the spherical movement of the dome above it, giving a smooth transition from the dome down into the square base of the space beneath. At the same time, the pendentive provides a tapering surface that is ideally suited to the display of painted or mosaic figures, and in the Byzantine church it became the conventional location for images of the four evangelists. The interior walls of the Byzantine church are largely covered with paintings or mosaics to fit the contours of the building, so that, as in the mosque (see pp.96–7), ornamentation is inseparable from structure.

The Gothic style, which developed in France in the 12th century and spread through most of western Europe, strives toward a similar effect but achieves it in a very different way. Both Gothic and Byzantine aimed to make walls more insubstantial, so that the building would emphasize space more than mass or surface. In each case, the engineering solution gave a different twist to the architectural expression

of Christian theology. In the Byzantine cathedral, heaven descends from the dome; in the Gothic, the gaze is swept upward to the forest of peaks where all vertical lines seem to meet. Whereas domes and circular arches are limited in size to their circumference, the pointed Gothic arch can reach any height, so that the sense of movement begins from the very bottom. Whereas the Byzantine overcomes the solidity of walls by using pendentives so that the dome appears to float in space, the Gothic makes walls thinner and breaks them up into bays through the use of buttresses. These remove part of the load-bearing mass to the exterior of the building and allow the height of the nave to reach more than three times its width. In the Byzantine style, windows around the base of the dome are often used as the main source of light, to enhance the heavenly effect. In the Gothic, the gaps that buttresses allow in the outside wall are used for windows that flood the interior with coloured light (see pp.50–51).

The undercroft of Fountains Abbey, Yorkshire, (mid-12th century), the earliest Gothic building in England and one of the earliest anywhere in Europe. As with Romanesque arches (see p.165), each leg stands at the junction of four vaults. But because of the strongly drawn diagonal ribs, each pillar is surrounded by a bundle of eight shafts. The criss-crossing ribs of the Gothic vault lead in an interlocking web from one bay to the next.

BUILDING WITH HUGE STONES

Some of the largest sacred monuments were constructed with the most basic technology. The details of the techniques often remain largely unknown, but the effort required to build these structures is testimony to the faith and determination of their builders.

At Stonehenge in England, sandstone boulders (known as sarsens) weighing up to c. 50 tons were brought from 20 miles (35 kilometres) away, probably on sledges or wooden rollers pulled by humans and perhaps animals. Once arrived, they were prepared using stone hammers. The lintels were slightly curved on the inside so that when they were joined they formed a complete circle; each was fixed to its neighbour by a V-shaped groove. Owing to the slope of the site, the height of the uprights was graded so as to make the circle of lintels absolutely horizontal.

The raising of these massive stones suggests extensive previous experience. The uprights were probably manoeuvred into place by ropes and levers, with the base of each stone levered into its hole and the whole stone hauled upright. Raising the lintels was much more difficult. They were probably levered level by level up a scaffolding, with logs jammed underneath to raise them at alternate ends.

In Egypt the builders of the pyramids relied on similar techniques. Massive blocks of stone were floated downriver when the Nile was in flood and hauled on sledges for the remaining short distances. These sledges were pulled along either on top of log rollers, or over ground on which water had been poured to reduce friction.

The stones had to be raised to an enormous height, and this too was accomplished entirely by human muscle-power. The great pyramids at Giza (see pp. 148–9) were built from the bottom up and finished from the top down. The core of the pyramid was built in steps, like the earlier step pyramids. Stones were hauled from one step to the next up ramps of earth and brick. Each course of stones was laid on a square platform and itself provided the square base for the next course. The pyramid was finished with a granite capstone. The outer surface was made of gleaming white limestone, of which only a little survives today, at the top of Khafre's pyramid. The outer casing stones were held together by matching joints which seem to have been carved on the ground beforehand. The joints were coated in mortar as a lubricant before the massive sloping stones were manoeuvred into position. Finally, the blocks were dressed layer by layer downward from the top and the ramps were dismantled.

Glossary

Words in SMALL CAPITALS
within an entry are cross-
referred

ambulatory a walkway around
the APSE of a church or
around a shrine; the covered
walk of a CLOISTER

apse a vaulted semicircular
alcove, such as at the end of
a Roman BASILICA or behind
the SANCTUARY of a Christian
church

archetype an original model
after which other similar
things are patterned; a
perfect or typical example

architrave a main beam laid
across pillars, used in
classical architecture; see
also ENTABLATURE, FRIEZE,
LINTEL, TRABEATE

axis a notional line, often
vertical, about which parts of
a building are arranged

baldachin a hemispherical
ceremonial canopy usually
above an altar; a dome in the
form of such

barrel vault an arched ceiling or
roof forming half a cylinder

basilica in Roman architecture,
a large meeting-hall, usually
rectangular, lit by a
CLERESTORY; the form was
taken up in early Christian
churches

buttress a projecting structure,
usually of masonry, that
strengthens or supports a
wall or building

capital the top part of a
column; see also CORINTHIAN,
DORIC, IONIC, ORDER

cardinal directions the four
principal directions on a
compass: north, south, east
and west

cathedral the principal church
in a bishop's diocese,
containing the bishop's
throne (*cathedra*)

chaitya an Indian Buddhist

temple – often a cave-temple
carved out of a cliff, with
aisles, and decorated with
sculpture

chancel the area around the
main altar in a church, often
containing seats for the choir
and reserved for the clergy
and choir; see also
SANCTUARY

clerestory an upper section of
a wall, containing windows
that admit light to a hall; see
also BASILICA

cloister a covered, arcaded
passage surrounding a
courtyard, often linking a
church and a monastery

corbel a projection of wood
or masonry (often stepped)
from a vertical wall,
supporting a weight

Corinthian the Corinthian
ORDER of classical
architecture, characterized by
slender, fluted columns with
elaborate CAPITALS decorated
with carved acanthus leaves;
see also DORIC, IONIC

cosmogram a diagram of the
structure of the world or
universe; see also *MANDALA*

crypt an underground room or
story beneath the main floor
of a religious building, often
holding relics or tombs

dolmen a prehistoric tomb
made of large upright stones
topped with a horizontal
stone, and originally buried
under a mound of earth

Doric the Doric ORDER of
classical architecture,
characterized by heavy, fluted
columns with plain, bowl-
shaped CAPITALS; see also
CORINTHIAN, IONIC

elevation a drawing of a vertical
plane or façade of a building;
see also plan, section

entablature in classical
architecture, a decorated
horizontal beam supported

by columns, incorporating
the three layers of
ARCHITRAVE, FRIEZE and
cornice

finial the crowning ornament
of a pinnacle, spire or dome

flying buttress a sloping or
arched BUTTRESS, typical
Gothic architecture, in which
the outward thrust of the
upper part of a wall is
transferred to the lower
support of the buttress

frieze a horizontal layer of
decoration; in the Greek
classical ORDERS the middle
layer of the ENTABLATURE

gopuram in southern India, a
tower-gateway of a temple

Greek cross a cross with four
arms of equal length, often
used in the design of
Christian churches; see also
LATIN CROSS

henge large, upright stones or
posts set in a circle, such as
Stonehenge

hogan a traditional North
American Navajo dwelling,
usually constructed of logs
and earth

hypostyle hall a large hall with
a flat roof supported by
pillars, especially in ancient
Egyptian architecture

iconostasis in a Greek or
Russian Orthodox church, a
screen used to display icons,
usually situated in front of
the altar and separating the
area of the church open to
the laity from that reserved
for the clergy

Ionic the Ionic ORDER of
classical architecture,
characterized by fluted
columns with scroll-like
CAPITALS; see also
CORINTHIAN, DORIC

Latin cross a cross with a long
upright traversed above the
middle by a shorter
crossarm; often used in the

design of Christian churches; see also GREEK CROSS

lintel a horizontal beam or stone over an opening, usually carrying the weight of the wall above it

mandala in Hinduism, Buddhism and Jainism, a stylized diagram of the universe based on a circle and a square, used as a meditational device and as the ground-plan for temples

megalith a massive stone used in prehistoric cultures for building, or on its own as a monument

menhir a single upright monumental stone, dating from prehistoric times

metope in the FRIEZE of a DORIC temple, a plain or carved panel between two TRIGLYPHS

mihrab a niche in the wall of a mosque or other Muslim building, facing Mecca and indicating the direction of prayer

minaret the high narrow tower of a mosque used for calling the faithful to prayer

monolithic shaped from a single block of stone

mosaic pattern formed by small pieces of coloured glass or stone set in mortar or plaster

Mount Meru in Hindu, Buddhist and Jain belief, the AXIS of the cosmos – a mountain at the centre of the world, often believed to link different layers of the universe

nave the main, longitudinal body of a Christian church from the western entrance to the TRANSEPT

necropolis a city of the dead, a large cemetery, especially in the ancient world

obelisk a tall, four-sided, usually MONOLITHIC stone, tapering to the top and ending in a pyramid shape

omphalos navel; a central or focal point, usually of the world or the cosmos

order the styles of building in classical architecture that are distinguished primarily by the CAPITALS at the top of their columns. The three Greek orders are, chronologically, DORIC, IONIC and CORINTHIAN; the Romans also used the Tuscan and the Composite

pagoda in the Far East, a development of the Buddhist *STUPA*, consisting of a tower with several stories usually diminishing in size as they ascend

passage-grave a prehistoric tomb in the form of a roofed stone corridor buried under an earth mound; also called gallery-grave

pendentive a curved triangular surface forming a junction between a dome and its supporting pillar or wall

peristyle a row of columns surrounding a courtyard or, as in the Greek temple, the exterior of a building

plan a drawing a horizontal plane of a building, as if seen from above; see also ELEVATION, SECTION

puja in Hinduism, Buddhism and Jainism, the ritual of worship and offering

pylon the massive gateway to an ancient Egyptian temple, comprising pairs of rectangular, truncated towers with sloping walls, on either side of the entrance

reredos an ornamental screen of wood or stone behind a Christian altar, often used to display paintings or carvings

sanctuary the sacred area around the main altar of a Christian church; see also CHANCEL

sarcophagus Greek "flesh-eating stone"; an elaborate coffin, usually of stone, often inscribed or decorated with sculpture or paintings

section a drawing of an imagined slice through a building along a vertical plane; see also ELEVATION, PLAN

shikhara a tower or spire of a Hindu temple, often tapering

step pyramid an early pyramid ascending in stepped terraces to a flat top

stupa a domed or pointed structure containing relics or marking a holy site, as a Buddhist memorial

tipi a conical tent of buffalo hide traditionally used by Plains and some other peoples of North America; also spelled tepee

trabeate an early type of construction using upright posts and horizontal LINTELS rather than arches or VAULTS; used for example in Egyptian and Greek temples

transept the transverse arms of a LATIN-CROSS church, usually shorter than the main hall formed by the NAVE, SANCTUARY and APSE

triglyph in a DORIC temple, a panel with three vertical grooves, alternating with METOPES in the FRIEZE

vault an arched ceiling or roof

yurt a single-roomed dwelling of the native peoples of Central Asia, usually round or polygonal in shape, easily movable, and with a central smoke-hole in the roof

ziggurat an ancient Mesopotamian temple tower in the form of a STEP PYRAMID, usually having a shrine at the top

Further reading

The literature in the field of sacred architecture worldwide is enormous, and mainly consists of general overviews on the one hand, and detailed studies of a particular tradition or site on the other. No author can be personally familiar with all these regions and we are indebted to a much wider range of sources than can be given here. We have listed our main specialist sources, along with some other books, both specialist and general, which we hope the reader will find useful. Where our treatment of a specific topic is particularly indebted to a work, the topic or spread-title is given in square brackets.

Certain encyclopedias (such as Eliade or Hastings) are a rich source of information on many aspects of sacred architecture, as is the scholarly journal *History of Religions*. Good histories and descriptions of particular buildings can often be found in tourist guidebooks and locally produced pamphlets.

Some of the titles listed (for example, Kramrisch or Mus) may be hard to find, but they are included because they are monumental original studies which are repeatedly quoted (sometimes inaccurately) in other more general works. Some titles exist in various reprints or editions.

Ardalan, N. and Bakhtiar, L. *The Sense of Unity: the Sufi tradition in Persian architecture*, University of Chicago Press, Chicago, 1973

Aveni, A.F. *Skywatchers of Ancient Mexico*, University of Texas, Austin and London, 1980 [alignments, astronomy]

Bloch, M. *Placing the Dead: tombs, ancestral villages and kinship organisation in Madagascar*, Seminar Press, London, 1971

Bloomer, K.C. and Moore C.W. *Body, Memory and Architecture*, Yale University Press, New Haven, 1977

Bourke, J. *Baroque Churches of Central Europe*, Faber, London, 1958

Braunfels, W. *Monasteries of Western Europe: the architecture of the orders*, Princeton University Press, Princeton, and Thames & Hudson, London, 1972

Brown, P. *Indian Architecture*, (2 volumes), Taraporevala, Bombay, 1956

Burl, A. *Prehistoric Avebury*, Yale University Press, New Haven, 1979

Carpenter, R. *The Architects of the Parthenon*, Penguin, Harmondsworth, 1970

Conant, K. *Carolingian and Romanesque Architecture 800–1200*, Penguin, Harmondsworth, 1973

Cowen, P. *Rose Windows*, Thames & Hudson, London, 1979

Daniel, G.E. *The Megalith Builders of Western Europe*, Hutchinson, London, 1958

Davies, J.G. *Temples, Churches and Mosques: a guide to the appreciation of religious architecture*, Blackwell, Oxford, 1982 [techniques of building]

Davies, J.G. *The Secular Use of Church Buildings*, S.C.M., London, 1968 [deconsecration]

Debuyst, F. *Modern Architecture and Christian Celebration*, Lutterworth Press, London, 1968

de Groot, J.J.M. *Chinese Geomancy*, Element, Shaftesbury, Dorset, 1989 [feng shui]

Denyer, S. *African Traditional Architecture: an historical and geographical perspective*, Heinemann, London, 1978

Dougherty, J. *The Fivesquare City: the city in the religious imagination*, Notre Dame University Press, Notre Dame, Indiana, 1980

Eck, D.L. *Banaras, City of Light*, Knopf, New York, 1982; Routledge & Kegan Paul, London, 1983

Edwards, I.E.S. *The Pyramids of Egypt*, Penguin, Harmondsworth, 1947

Eliade, M. (ed.) *Encyclopedia of Religion*, (16 volumes), Macmillan, New York, 1986

Foster, R. *Patterns of Thought: the hidden meaning of the great pavement of Westminster Abbey*, Cape, London, 1991

Fox, M.V. (ed.) *Temple in Society*, Eisenbrauns, Winona Lake, 1988

Frankl, P. *Gothic Architecture*, Penguin, Harmondsworth, 1962

Germann, G. *Gothic Revival in Europe and Britain*, Lund Humphries, London 1972

Gimpel, J. *The Cathedral Builders*, Pimlico, London, 1993

Gomez, L.O. and Woodward Jr, H.W. *Barabudur: history and significance of a Buddhist monument*, dist. Asian Humanities Press, Berkeley, 1981

Guidoni E. *Primitive Architecture*, Abrams, New York, 1978

Gutmann, J. (ed.) *The Synagogue: studies in origins, archaeology and architecture*, Ktav, New York, 1975

Gutmann, J. (ed.) *The Temple of Solomon: archaeological fact and medieval tradition in Christian, Islamic and Jewish art*, Scholars Press, Missoula, Montana, 1976

Hammond, P. *Liturgy and Architecture*, Barrie and Rockcliff, London, 1960

Haran, M. *Temples and Temple-service in Ancient Israel*, Clarendon, Oxford, 1978

Harpur, J. *The Atlas of Sacred Places: meeting points of heaven and earth*, Cassell, London, 1994

Hastings, J. (ed.) *Encyclopedia of Religion and Ethics*, (13 volumes), Clark, Edinburgh, 1908–26

Heggie, D.C. *Megalithic Science*, Thames & Hudson, London, 1981

Heyden, D. and Gendrop, P. *Pre-Columbian Architecture of Mesoamerica*, Abrams, New York, 1975

Heydenreich, L.H. and Lotz, W. *Architecture in Italy 1400–1600*, Penguin, Harmondsworth, 1974

Huntley, H.E. *The Divine Proportion*, Dover, New York, 1970

James, E.O. *From Cave to Cathedral: temples and shrines of prehistoric, classical and early times*, Thames & Hudson, London, 1965

Kostof, S.A. *A History of Architecture: settings and rituals*, Oxford University Press, Oxford, 1995

Kramrisch, S. *The Hindu Temple*, (2 volumes), University of Calcutta, Calcutta, 1946 [mandalas]

Krautheimer, R. *Early Christian and Byzantine Architecture*, Penguin, Harmondsworth, 1965

Kuban, D. *Muslim Religious Architecture: the mosque and its early development*, Brill, Leiden, 1974

Lawlor, R. *Sacred Geometry*, Thames & Hudson, London, 1992

Lawrence, A.W. *Greek Architecture*, Penguin, Harmondsworth, 1984

Lethaby, W. *Architecture, Mysticism and Myth*, Architectural Press, London, 1974 (first edition 1891)

Lundquist, J.M. *The Temple: meeting place of heaven and earth*, Thames & Hudson, London, 1993

Lyle, E. (ed.) *Sacred Architecture in the Traditions of India, China, Judaism and Islam*, Edinburgh University Press, Edinburgh, 1992

Mann, A.T. *Sacred Architecture*, Element, Shaftesbury, England, 1993

Marc, O. *Psychology of the House*, Thames & Hudson, London, 1974

Meyer, J.F. *Peking as a Sacred City*, Chinese Association for Folklore, Taipei, 1976

Michell, G. (ed.) *Architecture of the Islamic World*, Thames & Hudson, London, 1978

Mirsky, J. *Houses of God*, Constable, London, 1965

Moholy-Nagy, S. *Native Genius in Anonymous Architecture*, Horizon, New York, 1957

Morgan, L.H. *Houses and House Life of the American Aborigines*, Chicago University Press, Chicago, 1965 (first edition 1881)

Mus, P. *Barabudur: esquisse d'une histoire du bouddhisme fondée sur la critique archéologique des textes*, (2 volumes), Arno Press, New York, 1978 (first edition 1935)

Nabokov, P. and Easton, R. *Native American Architecture*, Oxford University Press, New York and Oxford, 1989 [Pawnee earth lodge]

Nitschke, G. "Building the sacred mountain: Tsukuriyama in Shinto tradition", in John Einarsen (ed.) *The Sacred Mountains of Asia*, Shambhala, Boston and London, 1995

Norberg-Schultz, C. *Existence, Space and Architecture*, Praeger, New York, 1971

Norberg-Schultz, C. *Meaning in Western Architecture*, Studio Vista, London, 1975

Nuttgens, P. *The Story of Architecture*, Phaidon, Oxford, 1983

Oliver, P. (ed.) *Shelter, Sign and Symbol*, London, Barrie & Jenkins, 1975

Oliver, P. *Dwellings: the house across the world*, Oxford, Phaidon, 1987 [Dogon; Kabylie]

Parish, S.M. *Moral Knowing in a Hindu Sacred City*, Columbia University Press, New York, 1994 [sacrifice; inner and outer realms]

Paine, R.T. and Soper, A. *The Art and Architecture of Japan*, Penguin, Harmondsworth, 1975

Paul, R. "The Sherpa Temple as a Model of the Psyche", *American Ethnologist*, 3:131–46 (1978)

Pevsner, N. *An Outline of European Architecture*, Penguin, Harmondsworth, 1960

Purce, J., *The Mystic Spiral: journey of the soul*, Thames & Hudson, London, 1974 [labyrinths and spirals]

Prussin, L. *Hatumere: Islamic design in West Africa*, University of California Press, Berkeley and London, 1986 [anthill-shaped mosques]

Renfrew, C. (ed.) *The Megalithic Monuments of Western Europe*, Thames & Hudson, London, 1983

Ringis, R. *Thai Temples and Temple Murals*, Oxford University Press, Singapore, 1990

Roux, G. *Ancient Iraq*, Penguin, Harmondsworth, 1975

Rudofsky, B. *Architecture without Architects: a short introduction to non-pedigreed architecture*, Doubleday, New York, 1969

Rykwert, J. *On Adam's House in Paradise: the idea of the primitive hut in architectural history*, Museum of Modern Art, New York, 1972

Rykwert, J. *The Idea of a Town: the anthropology of urban form in Rome, Italy and the ancient world*, M.I.T. Press, Cambridge, Mass. and London, 1976

Scully, V. *The Earth, the Temple and the Gods: Greek sacred architecture*, Yale University Press, New Haven, 1979

Shulman, D.D. *Tamil Temple Myths*, Princeton University Press, Princeton, 1980

Sickman, L. and Soper, A. *The Art and Architecture of Japan*, Penguin, Harmondsworth, 1975

Smith, B. *The Dome: a study in the history of ideas*, Princeton University Press, Princeton, 1978

Smith, J.Z. *Map is not Territory: studies in the history of religions*, Brill, Leiden, 1978

Smith, W.S. *The Art and Architecture of Ancient Egypt*, Harmondsworth, Penguin, 1971

Soper, A. *The Evolution of Buddhist Architecture in Japan*, Princeton University Press, Princeton, 1942

Stein, B. (ed.) *The South Indian Temple*, Vikas, New Delhi, 1978

Steinhardt, N.S. *Chinese Traditional Architecture*, The China Institute in America, China House Gallery, New York, 1984

Stierlin, H. *Encyclopedia of World Architecture*, (2 volumes), Macmillan, London, 1977 [techniques of building]

Stierlin, H. *The Art of the Maya*, Macmillan, London, 1981

Thomas, N. *Oceanic Art*, Thames & Hudson, London, 1995 [sacred meeting-place]

Tompkins, P. *Mysteries of the Mexican Pyramids*, Thames & Hudson, London, 1976

Tompkins, P. *Secrets of the Great Pyramid*, Harper & Row, New York, 1971

Tucci, G. *The Theory and Practice of the Mandala*, Rider, London, 1961 [mandalas]

Turner, H.W. *From Temple to Meeting House: the phenomenology and theology of places of worship*, Mouton, The Hague, 1979 [dwellings of the gods]

Vale, L.J. *Architecture, Power and National Identity*, Yale University Press, New Haven, 1992

Vitebsky, P. *Dialogues with the Dead: the discussion of mortality among the Sora of eastern India*, Cambridge University Press, Cambridge, 1993 [megaliths]

von Simson, O. *The Gothic Cathedral: origins of Gothic architecture and the medieval concept of order*, Bollingen, Princeton, 1988

Volwahsen, A. *Living Architecture: Indian*, Macdonald, London, 1969

Waterson, R. *The Living House: an anthropology of architecture in South-East Asia*, Oxford University Press, Singapore, 1990 [Nias; Toraja]

Wheatley, P. *The Pivot of the Four Quarters: a preliminary enquiry into the origins and character of the ancient Chinese city*, Aldine, Chicago, 1971

Wheeler, M. *Roman Art and Architecture*, Thames & Hudson, London, 1964

Index